"I think anyone considering homeschooling for their family will walk away from this book with the confidence to step forward and the tools to put it in motion. And those seeking to understand a friend or family member's homeschool decision will find themselves better informed and able to see it in a new way."

—Katie, stay-at-home mom of three public-schooled children

"In a systematic and logical way, based on research, Sandy addresses all the fundamental worries I had this year (our first as a homeschooling family). I have newfound confidence in my role as a home educator and my ability to respond to any potential criticism of our choice to home educate our children."

—Kristen, first year homeschooling mom of three

"LOVE IT!! Love the writing style, love the snippets of humor & pop culture, love that the white elephant in the room, referred to as "weird homeschooled kids," is addressed. I appreciate that the intention of the book is to open the eyes of parents to other educational options for their children. What a great way to gently challenge parents to make education a priority instead of an afterthought."

—Sheri, full-time brand and product development manager

"Parents and grandparents—this book is a must read! It's filled with valuable insights and personal examples presented in a very engaging writing style. I only wish this book was available when my children were growing up!"

—Shirley, grandmother of homeschooled and private-schooled children

"As a mom of three, I'm regularly considering our schooling options. *Think About Homeschooling* gives a clear picture of homeschooling and its far-reaching potential for many types of families. I'm so thankful for this great resource and really enjoy Sandy's witty writing style, too!"

—Beth, stay-at-home mom of a toddler and two private-schooled children

"After 15 years of homeschooling, I didn't think I needed another book on the subject. I was wrong! This book has reminded me of the importance of being able to explain why our family homeschools... not just for outsiders but, most importantly, for us."

—Jean, professional musician and veteran homeschooling mom

"Sandy provides real-life advice showing how practical and natural homeschooling can be for parents. Reading *Think About H~~~~~* ' ' a good chat with a friend over coffee that 3 journey."

nom of three

"I wish this book had been available when I was starting out as a homeschooler many years ago. Sandy is honest, transparent, and objective about every aspect of homeschooling, including some I didn't even know I should be thinking about until I ran into them myself. An excellent overview of what homeschooling is (and isn't) and why it just might be the best choice for your family."

—Kathy, part-time book editor and veteran homeschooling mom

"I've lived through seven decades of making choices and found myself on the proverbial fence many times. If you are in that position—thinking about homeschooling your children—this book will be a valuable resource. The author gives solid, practical advice in a user-friendly style, while presenting the core attributes of homeschooling and what they mean for you and your children."

—Henry, retired college instructor, corporate supervisor, and grandfather to homeschooled children

"I love that the author took us through her own journey of discovering the wonderful world of homeschooling. She offers this schooling option and demonstrates how accessible it truly is to everyone. The humor and relatable stories she presents help to ease any doubts or qualms a new homeschooling parent may have going in. Once you are done with this book, you come out the other side more confident, hopeful, and equipped to help your children follow their hearts and their purpose."

—Brook, part-time photographer and homeschooling mom of two

"A must read for anyone who wants to homeschool their children. I wish my mom had this resource when I was homeschooled 30 years ago."

—Lisbeth, homeschool graduate and pricing analyst

Think About Homeschooling

What It Is, What It Isn't, & Why It Works

Sandy Glenn

Sensible Life PUBLISHING

ISBN 978-1-7368430-0-0 (paperback)
ISBN 978-1-7368430-1-7 (ebook)

Library of Congress Control Number: 2021905051

First paperback edition April 2021

Edited by Lindsay Evermore
Cover and interior design by Christi Beem

Sensible Life
PUBLISHING

Dedication

This book is dedicated to my kids, without whom our homeschool wouldn't be nearly as fun and interesting as it is. I thank God for you and I love you all bunches!

Contents

Acknowledgements

First and foremost, I thank God for planting the seeds for this book in my mind and heart. Time after time, He made ways for this project to happen. One of the key provisions He gave me was the overwhelming support of my family and friends. So many people helped make this book possible and I'm grateful to them all!

Special thanks to:

- My husband and kids—Your patience throughout this process has been incredible and very much appreciated.
- My parents, Ross and Roberta—Thanks for all of your editorial suggestions, support, encouragement, and babysitting.
- My sister, Christi—Thank you for your incredible design work, professional input, and sisterly support.
- My brother-in-law, Eric—Thank you for steering me in the right direction with your early feedback.
- Lindsay Evermore—I'm so glad we connected for this project! Thanks for your skillful editing and helpful perspective.
- Robin Umbarger—I appreciate your keen eye and detailed proofreading. Thank you!
- Maricay Willis—Thank you for being my sounding board and for your feedback and ideas throughout the design process.
- Kathryn Olson—Thank you so much for your encouragement when this book was just a fledgling idea. I appreciate you reading my early manuscript, and I'm grateful for your advice.
- Kirk Smith, executive director of Illinois Christian Home Educators (www.iche.org)—My sincere thanks to you for reading my book and supporting this endeavor!
- Brian D. Ray, PhD, president of the National Home Education Research Institute (www.nheri.org)—Thank you for the time you spent reviewing NHERI statistics and references.
- My launch team and advanced copy readers—Your enthusiastic support in helping me get this book off the ground is something I'll never forget! Thank you all so much!

1

The Backstory

"I would *never* do that to my kids!" a neighbor exclaimed with shock and contempt as our young kids played within earshot. Just prior to her comment, I could've sworn I'd said we were homeschooling our oldest son for kindergarten. But based on her tone and the look of disdain in her eyes, you'd have thought I'd said we were planning on painting him purple and hanging him from a tree by his big toes.

As a new homeschooling mom, and as a person who is generally uncomfortable with conflict, I was unprepared for this reaction. With all the confidence I could muster, I mumbled something about it "working out okay for our family so far" and tried, unsuccessfully, to change the subject. The woman continued her tirade, seemingly unaware that her comments were anything other than helpful observations.

"School was such an amazing experience for me! I would never deny my own kids that! I mean, what about prom?! And friends!" She was practically shouting now, "I want my kids to have *friends!* No way! I would *never* homeschool *my* kids."

Thankfully, one of the children did something distracting, taking the conversation in another direction. I don't recall anything else we talked about during that impromptu playdate in her yard down the block. My head was swimming with questions, rebuttals, and insecurities.

Although I wanted to defend my family's new decision to homeschool, especially in front of my kids, the words didn't come when I needed them. After my two boys and I were back home, the "I should've said ..." thoughts began haunting me. I should've said how flexible and awesome our homeschool days were. I should've told her about the relaxed nature walks and the afternoons of free play and cookie baking and reading aloud together. My kids and I were learning so much about the world and each other, and the school year had only just begun!

I should've said that we *do* have friends. After all, my kids and hers were playing together with each other right under our noses and had been all summer long. Do friendships not count unless they met at a school?

I should've told her that I've read that homeschooled kids often *do* attend proms. Besides, who makes pivotal decisions on methods of education—the very foundations of their children's academic lives and future opportunities—based on a single dance children may or may not attend (and may or may not enjoy) that takes place twelve years in the future on a single evening of their young adult lives?

Most of me wanted to say these things. However, there was a part of me—a small but not insignificant part—that wasn't so sure. It was the part of me that wondered whether I really am in my right mind. Am I just a well-meaning but unhinged control freak who is unintentionally ruining my children's futures? After all, school was a pretty good experience for me, too (except junior high, but that's another story). I was public-schooled during my entire educational career, and I turned out okay. Isn't traditional schooling a rite of passage? Isn't it an essential shared experience of childhood? Am I robbing my kids of a right to which they are entitled?

Do the friendships we make at our homeschool co-op "count"? What if we only see those friends every few days? Is it more beneficial to have a group of kids you learn with every day of the week? I wasn't so sure anymore. In those early months of my oldest son's kindergarten year, I was about as confident as a mouse at a cat family reunion.

The truth was that I'd never done this before. I *wasn't* sure it would work. I was defensive because I was scared, uncertain, and inexperienced. Comments and advice from well-meaning friends and neighbors would throw me for a loop and back again.

How could I defend this lifestyle when I'd only been living it for a month? Sure, it seemed to be going well so far, but how dare I—a loving, nurturing mother—use my own children as test subjects in this unpredictable experiment? Here I was, effectively claiming that I could successfully teach my kids every subject and every grade level without a teaching degree. Just who did I think I was?

And what if they *do* miss out on prom?

Let's Start at the Very Beginning

The memories above are a glimpse into our first official year of home-schooling, but I'd been researching home education ever since my oldest child was a baby. I was insecure and still questioning my sanity, but at the same time, I was beginning to think I may have stumbled upon an unbelievable parallel universe with the potential to change everything. Let's go back to the very beginning. As Julie Andrews reminds us, it's a very good place to start.[1]

Like most American students, I attended public school from kindergarten through high school. In kindergarten, I was predominantly focused on my immediate surroundings: my desk, my supply box (made from a cardboard soda carton covered in contact paper), and my very own backpack cubby. Inside my five-year-old "awareness bubble" were my teacher and a handful of the other students in my class, including a few new friends and Larry the crayon stealer (name changed to protect the guilty). The well-known Swiss cognitive psychologist Jean Piaget described this egocentric, limited awareness as a hallmark of what he called the "preoperational stage" of cognitive development.[2] Basically, that's a fancy way of saying that little kids think the world revolves around them. In fact, they aren't even aware of the rest of the world.

---

1. *The Sound of Music*, directed by Robert Wise (Los Angeles, CA: Twentieth Century-Fox Film Corp., 1965), DVD.

2. Barry J. Wadsworth, *Piaget's Theory of Cognitive and Affective Development: Foundations of Constructivism*, 5th ed. (White Plains, NY: Longman Publishers USA, 1996).

As I aged, I progressed through Piaget's remaining cognitive development stages. Throughout elementary school, as I entered the "concrete operational stage," I became increasingly aware of the other classes in the building. And, mainly through band and sports, I began to realize that there were other schools with classrooms throughout our town and in the surrounding neighborhoods.

In junior high and high school, now having crossed into Piaget's "formal operational stage" of development, I was a teenager capable of a more complete awareness of abstract relationships and external happenings. In other words, my "bubble" expanded even further as I became aware of kids like me experiencing an education similar to my own in schools all over the state and nation. I learned that there were also private schools which were, as I understood it then, for the rich, famous, or Catholic. I had even heard about specialty schools such as IMSA, Illinois Mathematics and Science Academy, where a few of my friends were consigned in high school, never to be heard from again (by me, anyway).

College broadened the horizons of my understanding of the American K–12 educational system even further, to the point where they (my horizons, that is) stayed for much of my young adulthood. Not being involved in the field of education or having any real interest or reason to research it further, I continued to think of primary and secondary school in terms of what I knew from my own experience. As I saw it at that time, there might be a few unique opportunities for some students to study abroad, enroll in gifted or remedial classes, or attend a specialty school, but on the whole, students attended a public or private school in their town. That's how education worked and that's what everybody did. Or so I thought.

Little did I know, my "educational worldview" would soon shift dramatically.

Transitions

In 2005, a few years after I graduated from college, my husband and I were married. Had you told me then what my life would be like today, I would never have believed you.

As a newly married young professional, I worked at a prominent design-build architectural engineering firm in Chicago, the birthplace of the modern skyscraper. By the time I became pregnant with our first child several years later, my architecture career was taking off at another successful commercial/industrial architectural firm in the Chicago suburbs. My husband and I wrestled with the idea of my leaving such a promising career, even if only temporarily, to stay home with our son. However, after he was born in 2009, it became clear to us that my path would, for now, be that of a stay-at-home mom.

The transition to "at-home mom" from "working woman" was quite an experience in and of itself, and it could be the subject of another book. In fact, it *is* the subject of many books. For example, author and psychologist Dr. Shannon Hyland-Tassava wrote a guidebook to help struggling moms through this transition; she even named her book *The Essential Stay-at-Home Mom Manual*.[3] I, for one, definitely would've appreciated a manual. It was as if my emotions, social life, identity, short- and long-term plans, and financial situation were all tossed in a blender, pureed, and then poured into my hands (more specifically, poured into the one hand that wasn't holding the baby) so I could try to put the bits back together in an orderly way. Suffice it to say, at least a full year passed before I began to truly embrace, and feel comfortable in, my new role at home.

By this point in my backstory, my upbringing had included a series of fairly common, suburban, middle-class experiences and opportunities: K–12 public schooling, undergraduate and graduate studies at a state university, professional career, and marriage. To top it all off, my husband and I were more than halfway to our average-American goal of having 1.93 children.[4]

All this is not to imply that any of the above experiences are inferior or superior to other paths (although I do recommend rounding to whole numbers when having children). But according

---

3. Shannon Hyland-Tassava, *The Essential Stay-at-Home Mom Manual: How to Have a Wondrous Life Amidst Kids and Chaos* (Seattle, WA: Booktrope Editions, 2011).

4. "Average Number of Own Children Under 18 in Families With Children in the United States from 1960 to 2020," Statista, accessed March 9, 2021, https://www.statista.com/statistics/718084/average-number-of-own-children-per-family/.

to all the benchmarks in my imaginary "Succeeding in Middle-Class America" handbook, I was right on track. Even despite my fumbling as I stepped out of the working world and into at-home mom mode, I eventually found community and fulfillment and was generally enjoying life.

The Rabbit Hole Appears

In order to be prepared for becoming a mom (as if that were possible), I had started reading many parenting "how-to" manuals, excited to begin this new adventure called motherhood. Once our beautiful baby boy arrived, my search for answers and advice continued, albeit a bit more frantically than before. Somewhere in the postpartum blur of sleepless nights and "mommy brain," I picked up the book *Bringing Up Boys* by Dr. James Dobson.[5]

In the thirteenth chapter, titled "Boys in School," Dobson explores some of the difficulties many boys have in traditional public school settings and how important it is to be intentional about selecting a schooling option in which your child can excel. About halfway through the chapter, Dobson states that "if we had to do it over again, Shirley [his wife] and I would probably homeschool our children." He goes on to explain some of the benefits of homeschooling, especially pertaining to boys who, for a variety of reasons, might otherwise be labeled negatively or not reach their full potential in public school.

The word leapt off the page at me. "Homeschool?" I wondered aloud to myself. Having been home alone with an infant for several months, I was used to having conversations aloud with myself, so I continued. "What's that? Is that something people do? I don't live on a farm or make my own bread and I don't own any blue denim jumpers—am I even eligible for this?"

Whether I'd heard of homeschooling in the past or constructed these mistaken stereotypes in that moment based on the term

---

5. James C. Dobson, *Bringing Up Boys: Practical Advice and Encouragement for Those Shaping the Next Generation of Men* (Carol Stream, IL: Tyndale House, 2001).

"homeschool" I honestly can't recall. But clearly, in my ignorance, my first thoughts about homeschooling were confused at best. Still, knowing that a successful author, who is a licensed psychologist with a PhD in child development, spoke so positively of home education was intriguing.

In the following weeks, the word "homeschool" haunted me. What was this unfamiliar concept? Why had I never known of this option before? Surely it couldn't be a legitimate thing. I was under the impression that there were essentially two paths: public school and private school. Did homeschooling fit with those in some way or was it something else completely?

Looking back, I see the first cracks in my former "educational worldview" appearing during this time. Perhaps I was more uninformed than most, but the idea that people could and would and did teach their children at home came as a shock to me. As I continued to read all I could find about the topic, I was equally surprised to realize that not only was homeschooling a choice but it might actually be a *plausible* choice. Peering deeper into the rabbit hole, it appeared that homeschooling might even be the *preferred* choice for some families.

What's Next?

Some things in life you just have to try personally in order to truly understand them. For example, as a high school student, it's hard to imagine what college life will really be like until you get there and live it. Similarly, it's difficult to explain to someone the life-altering effects of parenthood if they've never had kids. In the same way, choosing to homeschool is an entire lifestyle change and is often hard for non-homeschoolers to imagine. It changes the way you view and define learning and education. It changes the way you structure your days, weeks, and years. It changes your finances, your priorities, and many of your life choices. It changes your relationship with your kids and their relationships with each other. In fact, I'd be hard-pressed to think of any aspect of my life and our family's life that homeschooling *hasn't* changed.

My family has been on this home education journey for a number of years now, and the dramatic shift my own thinking has undergone in that time continues to amaze me. Today, I'm an insider in the world of home education that I had never known existed. I used to wonder about "those homeschooling people"; now I'm one of "them."

Through research and personal experience, I've found—and continue to find—clarity regarding the misconceptions that surround home education. Over time, the true benefits and freedoms available in this lifestyle have become more and more evident to me. As is true for many homeschooling parents, increased confidence through experience has allowed me to engage more fully in both the big-picture vision casting and the daily implementation of our homeschool.

In the remainder of this book, we will unpack the false notions about homeschooling that keep some families from trying to educate at home and keep others trapped and insecure as they attempt it. As we chip away at home education's mistaken identity and think through it together, its true advantages and compelling potential will become increasingly clear. It is my hope that this clarity will help you better understand the homeschooling friends in your life and decide whether homeschooling might be a good choice for your own family. If you're already homeschooling, I pray this book will build your confidence and encourage you as you continue on your journey.

2

"I'm the Boss ... Need the Info"

The impetus for this book is summed up in this chapter's title: "I'm the boss ... need the info." These words, uttered in frustration by the infamous Dr. Evil in the movie *Austin Powers: International Man of Mystery*,[6] show that even a super-villain knows he can't lead well with outdated, inaccurate, or incomplete information. A boss (or, more broadly, any leader or manager, including parents) needs accurate information to guide, and make wise decisions for, those in his or her care.

Hopefully, unlike Dr. Evil, villainous world domination isn't our aim here. However, parents and guardians of school-aged children *are* responsible for the well-being of their dependents, including their education. At the very minimum, it is our legal duty to ensure that children obtain an education, but, of course, there are numerous moral, spiritual, ethical, and civic reasons to provide a quality education to all children.

Ideally, the decision on means and methods of educating each child would be based on relevant personal information: individual temperament, preferred learning styles, interests, strengths, and weaknesses, to name a few. Situational factors—family environment, availability of resources, and community opportunities—should also

---

6. *Austin Powers: International Man of Mystery*, directed by Jay Roach (Burbank, CA: New Line Cinema, 1997), DVD.

be considered. All available educational alternatives would be evaluated in light of these factors, after which an informed conclusion could be drawn.

However, as I already briefly described, until I happened across the word "homeschool" in a parenting book, I was unaware that homeschooling was even an option. Although I may have heard the word in the past, it wasn't fully on my radar; for all intents and purposes, I was oblivious to homeschooling. How could I compare educational options if I didn't know what they all were?

If you've ever been sidetracked by a special promotion at a grocery store, you might know what I mean. Upon entering the store,

---

Without a clear picture of educational alternatives, including what homeschooling is (and what it's not), parents are limited in their ability to make a truly informed decision regarding their child's education.

---

you notice an aisle endcap displaying three kinds of cereal for sale. You choose your favorite of the three and put it in your cart. However, ten minutes later, you find yourself in the cereal aisle amidst scads of other cereal choices. You now see that two additional favorites are discounted, and several other options have regular prices less than the sale price of the box in your cart. You also notice a totally new variety of your kids' favorite cereal that you think they'd love to try.

Long analogy short, you're the boss, the Family Cereal Selector, but at first you didn't have all the info. Only after you researched *all* of your cereal options, thinking through the different variables such as cost, taste, and nutrition, were you able to make a more educated decision.

Maybe you stuck with your initial cereal choice. Maybe, after weighing all your options, you switched to another box that wasn't on the endcap. And maybe you got fed up with the whole thing and grabbed a container of oatmeal instead. Who has time for all this overanalysis anyway? But, as most of us would agree, it helps to know your options before being asked to make a decision.

Whether choosing among cereals or making a more important decision such as buying a car, picking a career, or selecting a method of educating our child, *we can't choose an option if we don't know it exists*. Additionally, if the options are shrouded in confusion due to innocent naiveté, outdated stereotypes, or unfounded criticisms, an accurate decision is even more difficult to make. Without a clear picture of educational alternatives, including what homeschooling is (and what it's not), parents are limited in their ability to make a truly informed decision regarding their child's education.

Choices, Choices

As I described earlier, many people often think of their school choices in fairly well-defined silos: public, private, or parochial. Increasingly, though, it seems that our educational options exist more on a continuum. Especially recently, as educational choice has continued to be a hot topic in the public square, more options are becoming more available to more families. Depending on your location, you may have access to your choice of public schools with vouchers, charter schools, magnet schools, a wide variety of specialty private or independent schools (each with a unique emphasis and mission), homeschooling, hybrid schooling, learning pods, work-study programs, virtual and online schools, and all manner of supplemental educational services and programs.

To make matters even more overwhelming for the already stressed parent, within these categories there are many variations. For example, let's take a look at the category of "independent schools." A quick search on the website of the National Association of Independent Schools (NAIS)[7] turns up 247 options in the New York and New Jersey areas alone. There are schools focused on secular studies, religious studies, dual-language instruction, international studies,

---

7. "NAIS Directories," NAIS, accessed December 12, 2020, https://www.nais.org/directories/ (search directory: "Find a School"; Search filter: "East - NJ / NY").

self-instruction/free-learning, experiential learning, gifted programs, military academies, and more. Even in more rural areas, there are often at least a few alternatives from which to choose, or other ways to access supplemental educational programs.

Likewise, the umbrella term "homeschool" also encompasses a wide range of philosophies and methodologies within the larger continuum of educational choices. Some of the most popular methods include classical, unschooling, Charlotte Mason, project-based, Montessori, Waldorf, and unit studies. Then, there are those of us—myself included—who use the "whatever works" approach which, in homeschool circles, is known lovingly as the "eclectic" method.

Moving even further away from well-defined categories, some families choose to incorporate more than one educational method for their child(ren), and their strategies might look different as the needs of the child and family change over time. One common approach is for families to select a private school in the early years followed by a public high school. Since our family has started homeschooling, though, I've seen and read about more "mixed methodology" than I'd ever imagined was happening.

For example, homeschooling families often join co-ops to supplement and enrich their learning opportunities and to connect with other homeschooling kids and parents. One well-respected co-op, with branches nationwide and even a few internationally, is Scholé Groups. Their communities all share common values, but each local group has the "flexibility to customize their practices to their unique settings."[8] Some of their groups meet once a week, while the group closest to my town has options to meet two, three, or even four days a week. This essentially provides a hand-picked, private school experience for, let's say, three days of the week, while allowing the family to enjoy the benefits of homeschooling on the other two days. For parents who are on the fence about home education because they need to keep their part-time job, a group like this might make it entirely possible to homeschool.

---

8. "What Is a Scholé Group?," Scholé Groups, accessed December 12, 2020, http://scholegroups.com/what-is-a-schole-group/.

Many parents supplement their child's schooling with tutoring or specialized instruction in areas of particular weakness, strength, or interest. "After-schooling" and "car-schooling" are becoming more commonplace as parents use the time available to them to provide additional instruction to their child. Sometimes (but definitely not always), local public schools, private schools, and homeschool groups will allow non-attending students to share resources or participate in certain classes or activities. A private-schooled student might join the public school's photography club, or a homeschooled student might attend an art class at the local private school. (As an aside, this "equal access" for students is a topic of much debate. Always research applicable laws and regulations and contact your local school district to determine what resources may or may not be accessible to your student.)

Knowledge Is Power

My apologies if the previous section was overwhelming. If you've been under the impression that your school choice was binary (that is, that your choices are public school or private school), finding out that you have dozens of options can be a bit much to swallow. When all is said and done, even if your family doesn't choose an alternative educational path, it can still be a very eye-opening exercise to research all that is truly available in your area.

I recall a college course I once took in industrial psychology. The professor described a research study in which two groups of adults were put in separate classrooms and given written assignments. In both rooms, an irritating background noise persisted through the course of the experiment. Before the subjects started their work, Group A was told that the noise was a mechanical noise and that it could usually be minimized by changing the settings on the control panel on the wall if it got too annoying. Group B wasn't given any of this information. Interestingly, Group A's stress levels and performance were much better than Group B's even though no one in Group A ever actually changed the mechanical settings to stop the noise. Just *knowing* they could make a change was enough for them to focus and relax.

In the same way, just *knowing* your options, *knowing* there are alternatives out there if you need them, *knowing* where to find them and how to access them is liberating and empowering. It allows us as parents and caregivers to make better-educated decisions. But, just as importantly, it gets us unstuck from groupthink and the follow-the-crowd mentality. It allows us to explore the gray areas, not just the black and white. From relatively small changes (such as switching public school classes due to student–teacher incompatibility) to larger leaps of faith (like homeschooling your sophomore so they can take advantage of an international volunteer opportunity), please know that you do have options.

God has given you the privilege and responsibility of nurturing the child(ren) He's placed in your care. You are the steward and it's your child's future at stake, so don't be fooled into thinking you have no say in the matter. When you've found a good educational fit for your child and family, it should not be because "that's what everybody else is doing." Rather, it should be because you've weighed the options available to you and chosen it.

Every Day Is Kids' Day (A Disclaimer)

This book should not be interpreted as advocating homeschooling as the only or best way to educate every child. On the contrary, as we just reviewed, there are *many* choices when it comes to the education of our children. This is one of the main themes in the following chapters. It is only when we accurately understand our options, or are made aware that we even have a choice, that we can make the best decision for our children as individuals and our family as a whole. There are many factors in each family's decision; it would be a gross oversimplification to suggest that there is a one-size-fits-all answer for everyone.

Additionally, this isn't intended to be an anti–public school or anti–private school manifesto. By addressing misconceptions and outlining potential benefits of homeschooling, my hope is to clarify what home education is and what it is not.

On Mother's Day and Father's Day, my kids have asked me why moms and dads get their own special days and why there isn't a "Kids' Day." I remind them that *every* day is essentially Kids' Day. Similarly, the vast majority of education books, research, public debate, and discussion are about public and, to a lesser extent, private schools. Much less frequently is homeschooling mentioned. Of course, this proportionally low coverage is understandable given that homeschoolers represent a small minority of the K–12 students in the United States.[9]

By celebrating mom on Mother's Day or recognizing dad on Father's Day, we don't diminish the value or importance of our children every day of the year. In the same way, by discussing approaches and benefits to homeschooling, we don't diminish the value or importance of the public or private schools. This in-depth look at homeschooling is just that: a closer look at a lesser-known, and frequently misunderstood, educational alternative.

Under Pressure

> *"How to Be a Mom in 2017: Make sure your children's academic, emotional, psychological, mental, spiritual, physical, nutritional, and social needs are met while being careful not to overstimulate, understimulate, improperly medicate, helicopter, or neglect them in a screen-free, processed foods-free, GMO-free, negative energy-free, plastic-free, body positive, socially conscious, egalitarian but also authoritative, nurturing but fostering of independence, gentle but not overly permissive, pesticide-free, two-story, multilingual home preferably in a cul-de-sac with a backyard and 1.5 siblings spaced at least two years apart for proper development also don't forget the coconut oil.*
>
> *How to Be a Mom in Literally Every Generation Before Ours: Feed them sometimes."*[10]

---

9. "Fast Facts: Homeschooling," National Center for Education Statistics, accessed March 8, 2021, https://nces.ed.gov/fastfacts/display.asp?id=91.

10. Bunmi Laditan, "How to Be a Mom in 2017," Facebook, May 1, 2017, https://www.facebook.com/BunmiKLaditan/posts/1899244270322560:0.

As this Facebook post by Bunmi Laditan of *The Honest Toddler* fame summarizes well, parents today have enough "mommy [and daddy] guilt" without the added stress of rethinking everything they know about education. Just like we don't typically stand in the cereal aisle analyzing the unit costs of every single product, we may not feel like we have the time or patience needed to open the Pandora's box of educational choices. The thought of taking time to research the schooling options in your area might not sound that exhilarating. Reinventing your entire mind-set regarding education, or taking a leap of faith into the unknown arena of "not what everyone else is doing," is daunting to say the least.

But this isn't just a question of Funny Bunny Fruity O's versus Choco-Chummy Peanut Puffs. *This is your child's education.* Finding the best fit for them now could have an enormous impact on their future, their feelings towards learning, and their relationship with you. This is an important issue, and I encourage you to keep an open mind and gather as much information as possible. Arm yourself with knowledge and seek answers to your questions so that you, as the "boss," will have the information needed to make the best choice for your family.

3

Still Misunderstood

The four Alden orphans in Gertrude Chandler Warner's *The Box-car Children*[11] were in a tough spot. Their parents gone, they found themselves homeless and alone in the world. Though they knew their paternal grandfather lived nearby, they were sure he wouldn't like them since they thought he didn't like their mother. So convinced were they that he was someone to be feared and avoided, they set up a semipermanent home in an abandoned boxcar in the woods rather than approach him.

Fortunately (spoiler alert), the children do finally reunite with their grandfather, learning that he is a trustworthy, caring gentleman who has been searching for them all along. Clearing up this misunderstanding opens the door to an exciting future for James Alden and his grandchildren as they experience numerous adventures and, more importantly, they find love and connection through their close relationship.

People fear what they do not understand. We see this phenomenon of human nature playing out in minor ways on a daily basis. The preschooler being asked to taste a new food insists that he doesn't like it despite having never tried it before. If not for his insistent parents, his aversion might prevent him from discovering what turns out to be his new favorite food. As adults, our fear often manifests

---

11. Gertrude Chandler Warner, *The Boxcar Children* (Park Ridge, IL: Albert Whitman & Company, 2010).

itself as procrastination to mask the anxiety we feel when faced with new circumstances or unfamiliar tasks.

Sometimes, our healthy concern or reasonable apprehension when facing a novel situation can protect us from danger. However, an unchecked and unwarranted fear of the unknown is all too often a root cause of significant misunderstandings, missed opportunities, discrimination, and even violence towards others different from ourselves.

Misinformation and baseless judgements were the hurdles the Alden children had to clear in order to realize the truth about their grandfather and make a sound decision regarding their future. In the same way, clearing up lingering misconceptions and clarifying mistaken notions about home education will be the first step towards learning what it really *is*.

Misinformation Hurts

Misconceptions are one type of wrong information. We think something is something it's not. We have outdated or inaccurate data. This can usually be corrected easily by obtaining more accurate information. In the example above, upon meeting their grandfather, Mr. Alden's grandchildren quickly realized their preconceptions were off base. In light of the truth, they were able to quickly adjust their thinking to the reality that their grandfather was a kindhearted man.

Bringing our discussion back to the topic at hand, if someone thinks homeschooling must be done using school desks and a chalkboard between 8:30 a.m. and 3:00 p.m., they are simply mistaken. This is an example of a misconception. This notion is easy to correct by demonstrating that homeschooling can, in fact, be done using any number of "classroom" setups or with no designated "school space" at all. Similarly, school hours are inherently flexible for homeschoolers. When confronted with this reality, the individual should have a relatively easy time broadening their mental picture of homeschooling to include this new knowledge.

Stereotypes are a related but different kind of misinformation. They may (or may not) be rooted in grains of truth, but they err when they attribute characteristics of a few to an entire group. A stereotype differs from erroneous information in a number of ways, not the least of which is its persistence in the face of reality. Where correcting factual inaccuracies can be relatively quick to do, stereotypes are judgements about groups of people that can take much longer—generations, even—to completely eradicate. Even after meeting individuals who defy the stereotype in question, it still seems part of our human nature to categorize and label people and groups in ways that are not always helpful and are often hurtful.

Looking back, I'm ashamed to say my first thoughts of homeschooling were judgmental and based on stereotypes. Initially, my mental image of a typical homeschooling family included two homesteading parents with eight children. They were all wearing matching homemade outfits and happily canning homemade blackberry jam in their kitchen. I've since learned that none of those features (e.g., having a large family, sewing ability, canning experience) are necessarily a prerequisite for—or a result of—homeschooling.

My homeschool stereotypes seemed harmless enough. After all, I didn't *dislike* the imaginary family in my head. In fact, I applaud the self-sufficiency of homesteaders. And I believe children are a blessing from the Lord; I have the utmost respect for parents who can successfully rear a houseful of them. And I love blackberry jam. I just knew that my life didn't look much like the image in my head. If my initial picture of Jack and Jill Homeschooler was representative of a homeschool lifestyle, then, according to my line of thinking at the time, I had no business even considering homeschooling as an option. Case closed.

It might have seemed as though my preconceptions weren't hurting anyone; I wasn't actively, or even passively, *anti*-homeschooling. I had no interactions with homeschoolers and never spoke to or about them. But in reality, my inaccurate notions and stereotypical thinking *were* harmful—harmful to my own family. Based on my errant ideas, my family almost dismissed a perfectly viable educational option without further consideration. In this case, harm wasn't necessarily being done to others in any obvious way, but harm *was* being done to my own family in the form of potential missed opportunities.

A Muddled Mess

Both misconceptions and stereotypes are sources of confusion when it comes to understanding homeschooling (or, rather, *mis*understanding it). Most often they show up jumbled together, a bit of inaccurate information here mixed with a label or two there.

The idea that homeschoolers aren't, or can't be, well socialized, for example, is one of the most common criticisms of home education. There are a number of factors underneath this preconception. This view is usually based on mistaken ideas of how homeschooling works and unclear definitions of clichéd words like "socialization." It also stems from stereotypes; mannerisms of a few shy or quirky homeschoolers, or the actions of individuals from decades ago during the underground era of the modern homeschool movement, have become the basis for labeling the entire group and have persisted to this day. In reality, homeschooled kids, just like any other group of kids, come in a wide range of personality types and experience a variety of social opportunities that form and shape their unique characters.

Although the homeschool movement is growing (even more so during and after the events of 2020), homeschoolers are still a small minority.[12] Those outside home education circles may only meet a few homeschooling families, who then become the default examples influencing that individual's opinion of the entire homeschool community.

Case in point, shortly after I first heard about homeschooling, I met a homeschooling family who exactly fit the stereotype in my head. They had it all: seven or eight kids, matching homemade dresses, and even a delicate mix of excellent manners and social awkwardness. At that point, they were the only homeschooling family I'd met, and it only served to solidify my preconceptions.

To complicate matters further, in addition to the judgments and confusion, there are also legitimate disadvantages and idiosyncrasies

---

12. "There are an estimated 4.0 to 5.0 million homeschool students in grades K-12 in the United States (or 7% to 9% of school-age children). There were about 2.5 million homeschool students in spring 2019 (or 3% to 4% of school-age children). ... The homeschool population had been growing at an estimated 2% to 8% per annum over the past several years, but it grew drastically from 2019-2020 to 2020-2021." Brian D. Ray, "Research Facts on Homeschooling," NHERI, accessed January 16, 2021, https://www.nheri.org/research-facts-on-homeschooling/.

of homeschooling that need to be carefully considered. For example, most home educators are working with significantly less money per student than are traditional schools. Later, we'll dig deeper into the financial impacts of homeschooling, but, for now, the point is that all choices have real advantages and disadvantages that need to be evaluated.

When real concerns, incorrect "facts," and stereotypical notions are combined, we end up with a muddled mess. How can we expect to draw conclusions about the feasibility of homeschooling as an educational option for our children if we have no accurate picture of what it is?

Based on my preliminary knowledge of home education, I almost dismissed the idea outright. Of course, we can't all be experts in everything, especially in things we've never experienced. Most of us had a traditional schooling experience and simply aren't familiar with any other options.

• • • ────────────────

How can we expect to draw conclusions about the feasibility of homeschooling as an educational option for our children if we have no accurate picture of what it is?

• • • ────────────────

If we were talking about misinformation when it comes to which ice cream to choose for dessert, it might not much matter (besides, we all know peanut butter chocolate is the right answer anyway). Certainly, when it comes to more weighty decisions such as a car or house purchase, we want to be well-informed consumers with accurate data. How much more, then, when it comes to something as significant as our children's education, is it our responsibility to make every attempt to eliminate fallacious information and equip ourselves with the truth about our available options?

Just like in the Alden children's situation, what's at stake here isn't a trifling matter. Nelson Mandela once remarked, "Education is the most powerful weapon which you can use to change the world."[13] At the end of the day, whatever educational option we decide upon, we want to rest assured that we've carefully weighed all our alternatives and based our conclusions on factual information, our family's unique situation, and every child's individual needs.

Five Flavors of Fallacy

A quick internet search for "homeschool myths" demonstrates just how much false information is out there regarding home education. The vast majority of the search result articles are written by homeschoolers who are trying to shed some light on their misunderstood lifestyle.

While there are dozens of homeschool stereotypes, criticisms, and myths, I've found that they all fall into at least one of five broad categories, which are briefly outlined here and will be explored in greater detail in the following chapters. These main categories are *opportunity, effectiveness, practicality, motives,* and *community.*

Opportunity

Without a classroom setting and the associated resources, can we really expect homeschooled kids to have opportunities for socialization, quality academic learning, and extracurricular activities? What about the sports and science classes that require specialized equipment or lots of participants? Do homeschoolers lose out on those?

Knowing the vast array of opportunities available to public- and private-schooled students, and presuming that most homeschooling families don't have access to the funding and facilities to provide those options, some believe that homeschooling simply can't come close to providing a well-rounded social life or an experience-rich education.

---

13. "Nelson Mandela 1918–2013: South African Statesman," Oxford Reference, 2017, accessed March 8, 2021, www.oxfordreference.com/view/10.1093/acref/9780191843730.001.0001/q-oro-ed5-00007046.

Effectiveness

Closely related to the preconceptions about opportunity is the notion that homeschooling cannot be as effective as traditional schooling. After all, teachers go through years of school and on-the-job training to excel in their fields. Can untrained, uncertified moms and dads really provide a comparable experience for their kids for every grade and subject? Many critics question whether homeschooled kids are learning the right things at the right times and whether they'll be well prepared for the real world. Does a homeschool diploma even count when it comes to college admission, job applications, and military service? These and other questions cause some to assume that homeschooling is inadequate as an educational method and ineffective in preparing children for their future responsibilities.

Practicality

Even if parents like the idea of homeschooling and think it has merit, they are often turned off by what can seem like insurmountable obstacles. Giving up half the family's income so one parent can stay home and teach? That's just not feasible. Spending all day, every day with your kids? That's crazy talk. Having zero free moments to pursue your own interests? How could anyone possibly make it work?

At first glance, it just doesn't seem practical. This rings especially true for those of us with access to great local schools, where "tuition" is already paid in the form of property taxes. Why reinvent the wheel? Our resources—time, money, energy, sanity—are precious and already often in short supply. Straining them further just doesn't make practical sense.

Motives

If someone feels that homeschooling is impractical, ineffective, and lacking in opportunity, then it tends to follow that the person will also question the motives of homeschooling parents. They might see home education as an extreme form of helicopter parenting. Surely fear, or an unhealthy need for control, must be behind this if parents are willing to subject their own children to what, in the critic's view, is a less effective education with few beneficial learning opportunities.

Even more extreme, a few critics feel that parents use homeschooling to mask ulterior objectives such as avoiding vaccination, hiding from "real life" (such as bullying) in an overprotective way, perpetuating religious brainwashing, or hiding lazy, neglectful parenting. These critics often argue that too much freedom is a dangerous thing and that more government regulation is needed to ensure the safety of children.

Community

The final group of critiques includes ideas related to community and social responsibility. Quality education benefits each individual but also our communities as a whole. For the sake of the homeschooled kids and the rest of us, shouldn't homeschooling be heavily regulated, or just done away with altogether, to ensure that certain standards are met? How will these isolated homeschooled kids, having had such dissimilar educational experiences, relate to their peers in the future as co-citizens of their communities?

Sure, the public school system is flawed, but doesn't that make it even more important for all families to work together to improve it? In secular and religious communities alike, critics argue that kids can't effectively reach out to their peers or help improve the traditional school system if they aren't a part of it. Some say that homeschooling parents are running away from the problems in their communities and sticking their heads in the sand instead of jumping in to make a difference for the better.

Not Everyone's a Critic

Listing all these criticisms in a row paints a one-sided picture of the public's view of homeschooling. While some people are critical of homeschooling, there are many supporters, even outside the homeschooling community, who understand its numerous benefits and appreciate its potential. As homeschooling increases in popularity, more and more non-homeschoolers are hearing about it, adjusting their understanding of it, and considering it as a viable option for others and their own families.

From my own anecdotal experience, I would estimate that the reactions I've gotten regarding our decision to homeschool are 60% positive or supportive, 20% curious or neutral, and 15% negative or unsupportive. The other 5% had no idea what I was talking about. Unfortunately, the negative reactions, despite being a minority, are the experiences we often remember vividly. That 15% can feel like a lot more if we aren't intentional about staying positive, maintaining our focus, and keeping things in perspective. Ultimately, we shouldn't allow others' perceptions and judgements to dictate our choices, but this can be very difficult in practice, especially in the face of bold opposition or negative pushback from close family and friends.

Through the following analysis of homeschool myths and misinformation, keep in mind that not everyone is a homeschool critic. Some are. But many are not. And many people, once they have a better understanding of what homeschooling is, become the movement's staunchest supporters. By talking through these questions and sorting out fact from fiction, we can all become better informed, more aware of our own preconceptions, and better prepared to address questions and criticisms when they do arise.

4

Opportunity for Socialization

"I worry in a lot of cases students who are home schooled are not getting the kind of breadth of instructional experience they would get in school. They're also not getting the opportunities to develop relationships with peers unless their parents are very intentional about it ... I do worry about whether home schooled students are getting the range of options that are good for all kids."
—John B. King Jr., former U.S. Secretary of Education[14]

In this quote from a Christian Science Monitor breakfast attended by former U.S. Secretary of Education John B. King Jr., we see several stereotypes and assumptions (which continue to persist despite evidence to the contrary), mixed with seemingly genuine concern and at least one very significant point. To be fair, within the same conversation, King also stated that "there are examples of [homeschooled students] doing incredibly well ..." and noted that he "had college classmates who had home schooled, and experienced tremendous academic success." Unfortunately, the context and wording of his comments suggests that, in his opinion, the success stories are the exception and not the norm.

---

14. Arianna Prothero, "U.S. Secretary of Education Weighs In on Growing Home School Numbers," *Education Week*, last modified September 22, 2016, https://www.edweek.org/policy-politics/u-s-secretary-of-education-weighs-in-on-growing-home-school-numbers/2016/09?qs=homeschool.

King mentions "breadth of instructional experience," "relationships with peers" (i.e., socialization), and "the range of options" to be aspects of a homeschool education where he feels opportunity is lacking. Although he didn't get into specifics on this occasion, other critics have, and we'll examine those instances in just a moment.

First, though, King makes a good point which you'll see woven throughout this book. The idea that opportunities for relationships are lacking "unless their parents are very intentional about it" is both true and critical to homeschool success. King is speaking about social opportunities, but the need for intentionality applies to all aspects of home education. By definition, homeschooling parents have taken educational matters into their own hands. They may choose to delegate parts of their job role in various ways, but intentional thought and planning is part of the responsibility that comes with homeschooling.

The "S" Word

Ugh … the dreaded "S" word. Socialization. The concept of unsocialized homeschoolers is the subject of books, magazine articles, memes, funny T-shirts, and blog posts. Websites like *www.unsocialized.net* and *www.weirdunsocializedhomeschoolers.com* use the idea as their namesake. There is even a podcast network called the Unsocialized Media Network serving the homeschooling audience. Although many homeschoolers are just plain sick of addressing it, I would be remiss if I didn't dedicate some time to discussing one of the top criticisms of homeschooling, as clichéd as it may be.

One of the first questions typically asked of homeschoolers is, "What about socialization?" During the beginning of my own educational worldview shift, I remember asking myself and other homeschoolers this question verbatim and truly not comprehending how homeschooled kids would socialize. Digging deeper into what "socialization" means was a pivotal first step in clarifying my own misunderstandings about homeschooling, so let's start there.

Defining Terms and Exposing Assumptions

Instead of asking, "What about socialization?" we should first ask ourselves, "What is socialization?" The definition on *Merriam-Webster.com* says that socialization is "the process beginning during childhood by which individuals acquire the values, habits, and attitudes of a society" or "social interaction with others."[15] Similarly, but not identically, *Dictionary.com* tells us that socialization is "a continuing process whereby an individual acquires a personal identity and learns the norms, values, behavior, and social skills appropriate to his or her social position."[16] To say it yet another way, there's a world out there, filled with people, and kids need to know how to live in it.

If, when asking, "Are homeschooled kids socialized?" a person was only checking whether the dictionary definitions were being fulfilled, homeschooling parents could simply say "yes," produce the appropriate proof—a résumé of clubs and activities or a completed social skills checklist for their age—and move on. Yes, they are being trained for social environments. Yes, they participate in groups. Yes, they're acquiring social skills. If that was truly the extent of the inquiry, it would be easy to answer. Yet, here we are, dozens of years after the modern homeschool movement began, still plagued by the idea that homeschooled kids are weird and unsocialized.

Clearly, there's more to this than dictionary definitions. In my experience, when a questioner asks, "What about socialization?" they generally mean some combination of more specific questions. Also, though they may be asking with the best of intentions, their inquiry is often based on faulty assumptions. Generally speaking, non-homeschoolers inquiring about homeschool socialization really mean one or more of the following questions (I've included their unspoken, inaccurate, underlying assumptions in parentheses):

---

15. "Definition of Socialization," Merriam-Webster, Inc., accessed March 8, 2021, https://www.merriam-webster.com/dictionary/socialization.

16. "Socialization," Dictionary.com LLC, accessed March 8, 2021, https://www.dictionary.com/browse/socialization?s=t.

- Will they be able to make friends? *(since they are at home alone with mom all day)*
- Will they know how to interact with other kids? *(since they are rarely around other children besides siblings)*
- Will they be different than public-schooled kids? *(since different is weird and weird is bad)*
- Will they know how to walk in line, wait their turn, raise their hand to speak, and so on? *(since those are critical, foundational social skills that help to keep order in our classrooms and society and can't be learned in any other setting)*
- Will they appreciate and respect other cultures? *(since they'll rarely be exposed to anyone different than their own family)*
- Will they know how to play with friends, share, and compromise? *(since, again, they'll only be around mom and siblings most of the time)*
- Will they have opportunities to participate in social activities such as group sports and theater? *(since parents simply can't provide the same opportunities available to traditionally schooled students)*
- Will they know how to interact with and respect authorities other than their parents? *(since their only teachers are their parents)*
- Will they be able to handle the people and pressures of the real world? *(since they've been isolated and overprotected by their parents)*

When we look at the possible underlying assumptions, it becomes apparent that the resulting questions come from simply not understanding what homeschooling is really like. The majority of the questions above stem from the assumption that homeschoolers have very limited interaction with the world outside the walls of their own home. Research, observations, personal experience, and anecdotal evidence all show this to be resoundingly untrue in the majority of homeschooling families.

DIY Socialization

Many resources have already been written that demonstrate, in detail, how homeschooling can and does provide ample opportunities for social interaction. In her book, *The Well-Adjusted Child: The Social Benefits of Homeschooling*,[17] Rachel Gathercole covers the topic in depth and discusses ways in which home education not only meets basic socialization needs but can also be *more* beneficial for healthy socialization than other options. Reading this, and other books like it, shifted my thinking dramatically and helped open my mind to the idea that there might be another equally acceptable way of doing things.[18]

Gathercole describes how she, like most of us, was conventionally schooled. She reflects on the moment her eyes were opened to a world beyond that which she knew. While observing a midday homeschool playdate, in which a park was "positively bustling with children" playing, talking, and laughing, she states, "I had never pictured that such things would, or even could, be going on in the world during school hours. In fact, I thought that school was the place where social life was—where friends were found, where life was centered—in short, where it was at." This is exactly the revelation I had when we started homeschooling as well.

Now, years later and surrounded by other homeschooling families, it baffles me how astounded I was that there was life happening outside the school walls during school hours. When we first got involved in our co-op and other homeschool activities, I remember thinking, "Where did all these people come from?" I had no idea there was such an active homeschool community in my town and surrounding neighborhoods. I had just never thought about it and hadn't thought to look for it.

In a short article on the PBS website,[19] author Bridget Bentz Sizer quotes Kate Fridkis, a blogger at *Skipping-School.com* who was unschooled, as she sums up the main issue. "People seem to translate the term [homeschooling] literally into 'school in the home' … but

---

17. Rachel Gathercole, *The Well-Adjusted Child: The Social Benefits of Homeschooling* (n.p.: Mapletree Publishing Co., 2007).

18. For additional reading on the topic of socialization, also see Susan A. McDowell, *But What about Socialization? Answering the Perpetual Home Schooling Question* (Nashville, TN: Philodeus Press, 2004).

19. Bridget Bentz Sizer, "Socialization: Tackling Homeschooling's 'S' Word," PBS, last modified October 25, 2011, https://www.pbs.org/parents/thrive/socialization-tackling-homeschoolings-s-word.

you're actually socializing so much more than your average kid who's sitting in class all day." I agree wholeheartedly, but it's often difficult for non-homeschoolers to visualize what this would look like or understand how her statement could be true.

Certainly, not all communities are the same when it comes to available enrichment opportunities, but, once we start looking, there is often more there than we had realized. Between park playgroups, church groups, camps of all kinds, park district classes, art and music lessons, intramural athletics, travel and team sports, fitness clubs, academic and enrichment co-ops, chorus ensembles, scouting groups, theater troupes, homeschool or community bands and orchestras, 4-H clubs, library classes, science and STE(A)M teams, community service, and volunteering, many neighborhoods have more available than any family would ever have time for. Even a town with a small fraction of these myriad extracurricular activities provides ample opportunity to meet others and connect with them around common interests.

In addition, many homeschoolers take advantage of art, music, gym, and academic classes at their local public or private schools. As we saw earlier, hybrid schooling options are becoming increasingly available, as are online classes and virtual communities. Clearly, any of these classes and learning situations would provide a source of peer interaction as well.

The main difference between traditional schooling and homeschooling, with regards to social opportunity, is that many aspects of public/private school socialization are "prepackaged," whereas homeschooling socialization tends to be more "DIY." When I showed up to my first day of kindergarten many years ago, there were a dozen or so other kids, all presorted by age, awaiting socialization. When my family started homeschooling, it took a little extra effort to sign up for a co-op, although this is not much different than what most non-home-educating parents do when searching and registering for preschool. It also took some time to think about the academic or enrichment classes we wanted to join to supplement our curriculum and provide social experiences of all kinds.

In the end, both my kids and I have built wonderful, lasting relationships in and outside of our homeschool community. My children have had diverse and plentiful chances to bond with peers and people of all ages. They've grappled with the delightful dilemma of having a birthday party guest list that's too long. In fact, many—myself included—would submit that, far from being a hindrance to socialization, homeschooling has afforded our kids *more* time and freedom to socialize in a wider variety of environments.

Ultimately, as King reminded us earlier, a large part of successful peer interaction opportunities comes down to intentionality. Due to the "prepackaged" nature of traditional schools, however, it's easy to overlook that *all* parents need to be intentional about the socialization of their kids. The fact that there are other kids in chairs next to your child by no means ensures that positive socialization experiences are occurring. Effort on the parents' part is required to stay "in the know" and provide age-appropriate social guidance, activities, and supervision when needed, regardless of the school their kids attend (or don't attend).

The efforts of the intentional public-schooling parent often don't look all that different than those of the homeschooling parent. Where a public-schooling mom might rearrange her work schedule to be room-mom twice a month, the homeschooling mom might be volunteering in a similar capacity at a homeschool co-op. A public-schooling dad might attend PTA meetings, while a home-educating dad attends parent planning meetings with his local homeschool support group. Regardless of schooling method, all parents share other common "family social duties" like planning a sleepover for their children and their friends, signing up for and chauffeuring kids to extracurricular classes, and planning birthday parties and playdates for their children. No matter how you educate your kids, providing healthy social interactions for them is part of your job description.

Wherever You Are, You Can Make Friends

Thinking back to elementary school, I recall being in a class of seven girls and fourteen boys. I had three close friends and several acquaintances (i.e., those close enough to invite to my birthday party but not close enough to trade secret notes with in class). The rest of the class I tried to avoid—there were too many "cooties" with the disproportionate number of boys around. Despite what the girls felt was an unfortunate gender ratio, school was where I made friends. Like Gathercole said, it was "where it was at." Only more recently have I realized that school was only "where it was at" for me because it was where *I* was at. In other words, if I'd been educated somewhere else, then *that* would've been "where it was at" for me.

Public schools aren't the only place to meet people. As I continue reminiscing about childhood relationships, I remember that some of

---

... No matter how you educate your kids, providing healthy social interactions for them is part of your job description.

...

---

my closest friends were neighbors not in my grade at school. Another friend and I met in an extracurricular summer enrichment class, and I befriended another girl in a summer sports camp. My first boyfriend attended a different high school altogether, yet he wound up in our group of friends. One of my closest and longest-enduring friendships was with a girl from my church; only years later did we end up at the same school together. Our kids now play together, too, even though we've chosen different schooling paths for them.

I encourage you to take your own trip down memory lane and think of the various places you've met friends. For real, go ahead. I'll wait …

Probably many of your friendships started in school, but were there also neighborhood kids you rode bikes with or played ball with in the driveway? Do you recall meeting peers in summer camp or on a park district softball team? Maybe you got to know your parents' friends' kids when your families got together for dinner. Maybe your best friend was someone from the community orchestra or the child whose mom babysat you after school. Did you make any friends at church or in your youth group? Did you ever meet anyone new on a vacation or at camp or anytime during the summer?

How about now? As an adult, where do you make friends? Work? Maybe, maybe not. Church? Your fitness center? Book clubs? Volunteering at the food pantry? There is an old adage that states "wherever you go, there you are." Hopefully the original author of this statement won't mind if I add a logical follow-up: wherever you are, you can make friends.

That's not to say it's always easy. Our family got off to a slow start the first year of homeschooling and it's only more recently, after seeing it work firsthand, that I can honestly say that the socialization doubts have truly been laid to rest in my mind. In the same way, though, the first year in a new public school after moving to a new neighborhood might be slow and painful at times (I can attest to that from personal experience as well). Joining any new group, switching churches, going away to college, starting a new job—any of these are situations where you might have those scary, awkward "new kid" feelings. It's always hard at first. But, remember, the very act of stepping off the beaten path and interacting with new people in new situations is, itself, excellent practice in socialization.

What's the Hang Up?

So, we've reviewed the list of places we can find peers and established that homeschooling families are able to find other human beings with whom to interact. Now what? Why do skeptics remain unconvinced even after we rattle off the stellar extracurricular résumé as proof of socialization? Why, in my first couple of years as a homeschooling mom, did I *still* have a nagging seed of doubt as to whether my kids would find true and deep friendships? If you're a homeschool critic who remains doubtful or a parent still wondering whether your child would feel isolated if homeschooled, try getting at the root of your reservations.

Perhaps you met a "weird homeschooler" and can't get past the stereotype. First, think about what you mean by "weird." Does weird just mean "different" or "unique"? If the weird homeschooler had been traditionally schooled, would that have made him less weird? Or are some people just atypical no matter what? Is it possible that given more time and freedom to pursue their individual interests and talents, there might be a higher proportion of "unique" or "different" hobbies and personalities displayed in the homeschool community?

If this impression of homeschoolers as "unsocialized" continues to nag you, try finding another homeschooling family (not the weird one you already met) or a homeschool conference to attend to challenge the stereotypical thinking. Look around at the many different people represented in the homeschool community. Interact with them and listen to their stories. Socialize with them!

Maybe your socialization concerns stem from a disability or unique personality trait that makes socializing difficult for you or your child. In this case, there will likely be extra intentionality needed on your part regardless of the schooling option chosen. Carefully weigh the social aspects of each method of education to find the social setting in which your child will thrive the most. Depending on the situation, an open-minded school counselor or therapist might be a good person to consult to determine whether the extra freedom and individualization possible in a homeschool setting would benefit your child. Try to think past the generalizations of "public school, private school, or homeschool" and get specific. Visit the public or private school your child would actually be attending to see whether the teachers and programs at *that* school would be a good fit. Share your concerns and see what accommodations might be available for your family's unique circumstances. Similarly, when looking into homeschooling, research the many different methods out there and try to begin building a mental picture of what *your* homeschool could look like.

For many of us, if we are honest enough with ourselves to really look at it, the root of our misgivings is fear. Fear of the unknown and of going against the societal grain are strong motivating factors. I know that fear of being different was the ultimate hurdle I had to jump before I was able to relax and move past my concerns about socialization. When I was the new kid on the block in second grade, my parents reminded me to just be myself and friendships would come. That advice holds true in this context as well. When we relax enough to let our true selves shine, to move forward on a path we know is right for our family regardless of societal pressures, it's then that we tend to find the deepest bonds with others.

Good and Bad Socialization

At this point, we've seen that homeschoolers have no shortage of places to be and that they can practice a variety of social skills in any of those places. Although all of this is true and necessary to understanding the question of socialization, it is only half of the equation. If the burden of proof is on homeschoolers to demonstrate that they get enough socialization, then it isn't unreasonable for parents to ask traditional schools to demonstrate the adequacy of *their* schools' social scene, too.

In any environment there will be both obstacles to, and catalysts for, social interaction simply based on the nature of the setting. For example, in a traditional school, much of the day is spent with same-aged peers. This can be looked at as a positive thing, providing chances for fair and healthy competition, enabling age-appropriate group teaching, and facilitating a more "even playing field" for peer interaction in physical skill–based classes like gym.

On the other hand, the age-segregated environment common to most public and private schools is foreign to the work and social environments found in the "real world" later in life (the nebulous concept of the "real world" is addressed in more depth in Chapter 8). Every hour spent in an age-segregated classroom is an hour not spent in a multi-aged classroom filled with an age spread more representative of their future workplace. Additionally, an hour spent in either of those classrooms is an hour *not* spent talking with an elderly neighbor, tutoring a younger sibling, or leading a mixed-age community book club. It may be the norm, but is the age-segregation aspect of traditional schools the only or best option in light of other possibilities such as multi-aged classrooms and intergenerational learning?

Other aspects of socialization that need to be considered are peer pressure, bullying, and school violence. These are mentioned frequently in the news and are the negative side to the socialization coin. Unfortunately, neither public, private, nor home-based schools are immune to these harmful issues. Wherever there is more than one person, there will always be the opportunity for both positive and negative interpersonal interactions.

Trying to find the balance between "too protective" and "not protective enough" is difficult for all parents. It's easy to criticize others for being a Helicopter Helen or a Laissez-Faire Linda. The unschooling family, guiding their kids with minimal parental interference, is labeled irresponsible and negligent. At the same time, the parents of the student pulled out of school due to an escalating bullying situation are condemned as overprotective.

———————————————————— ...

Wherever there is more than one person, there will always be the opportunity for both positive and negative interpersonal interactions.

———————————————————— ...

In any educational setting, building resilience in our kids is important, but so is safeguarding them. While the level of parental involvement in homeschools tends to mitigate some degree of school-related violence and peer pressure, age-appropriate supervision and guidance are important in all educational methods. Public-schooling parents can't abdicate their responsibility to train and protect their kids, and homeschooling parents shouldn't assume that their home-based education will eliminate these issues. It's important to know that there are both negative and positive sides to socialization and various ways you'll need or want to get involved as your student encounters them.

Think It Through

There are many other social components that should be evaluated when making an educational decision for children. For example, at some point, exposure to the "sex, drugs, and alcohol" side of socialization is inevitable. How, when, and by whom should those topics be introduced in order to protect kids while also empowering them to think for themselves? Does competition help or hinder learning? What are the best environments in which to practice the art of conversation or debate? Who do we want modeling manners and social graces to our children—parents or peers? The answers to these types of questions depend heavily on your worldview, family values, surroundings, and individual personalities and temperaments.

There is no one right setting best for the socialization of all children. Social interactions can and will happen wherever there are two or more people in the same physical or virtual space. What types and facets of socialization are important to your family, and how will you go about fulfilling them? Whichever educational path your kids are on, take a look at the pros and cons, the catalysts and obstacles to relationships they'll encounter, and determine how you'll make the most of the good and minimize the negative effects of the bad.

"I Will Remember You …"

Sarah McLachlan's tear-inducing ballad "I Will Remember You" was the theme song of my high school senior prom. With photo booths, professional photography, corsages from the florist, tuxedos and dresses that rival fine wedding apparel, not to mention the big-name bands and feasting, proms are certainly nights to remember! If the number and extravagance of prom proposals on YouTube alone is any measure, I think it's fair to assume that prom is very important to many high schoolers.

I also remember homecoming parades, quarterly school dances, choral and band concerts, football games with friends, and elaborate graduation ceremonies. These are, for the most part, wonderful memories for me. What are some of your favorite memories of your high school years? Were they magical? The best times of your life? Or would you rather put those days behind you?

These and other social milestones and events (or rather, the perceived lack of them) are often cited as a downside to the homeschool lifestyle, perhaps a part of the "opportunity" that King worries is lacking in the life of homeschooled children and young adults. The assumption is that these events simply aren't accessible to homeschooling families since they require more people, resources, and venues than most homeschoolers have at their disposal. How could the average Sally Homeschool Mom and her kids possibly recreate all of these experiences? The answer is that they can't. And they can. And they don't need to.

It's My Party ...

My own prom was a blast. Our group dined extravagantly before dancing the night away in the school gymnasium. Afterwards, we continued the festivities aboard a school-sponsored boat cruise on Lake Michigan (intended mainly to keep kids from post-prom shenanigans). Having the boundless energy and free spirits common to kids that age, our group then drove a few hours, in the middle of the night, to a state park for a deliriously exhausted but fun-filled day at the beach. The dance and cruise were arranged for us, but the dinner and post-prom day trip were planned by my friends and myself.

Similarly, as a tween, my sister used to organize themed parties. Her Mother & Daughter Soirée was a lovely girls' night gathering for her friends and their moms. At other events, like her Halloween Bash, her guests experienced creative entertainment like feeling "squishy eyeballs" (peeled grapes) and "gooey brains" (spaghetti) while blindfolded. And all this before the era of Pinterest! One of her most memorable events was her International Party, which boasted food, flags, music, and cultural displays for a variety of countries. The friends attending enjoyed activities and fun conversation over Mexican tacos and Czechoslovakian kolacky and may have even learned a thing or two. These events were fun for everyone involved, and all it took was a resourceful girl with creative ideas.

My sister was public-schooled, but she didn't wait for her class to study cultural awareness in order to host her celebration of nations. Supportive parents and friends, dollar store decorations, a little time, and a willing attitude were all she really needed to make her events successful. The world of homeschooling is no different. If an event is important to a student, family, or group, they can generally find a way to experience it. In many cases, the involvement and self-sacrifice required to create the event makes it even more memorable for the people involved.

We've discussed how *un*-isolated most homeschoolers are, so it's really not much of a stretch to imagine them organizing group events. (Side note: if the "socialization" topic is still a hang-up for you, I strongly recommend putting this book down and reading the books I mentioned earlier that have been written on that topic. Understanding that socialization is a nonissue is critical to rethinking all other aspects of homeschooling.) Co-ops often host graduation ceremonies, art shows, talent competitions, dances, and the like. Homeschool groups in some states host large-scale events such as statewide proms and outings like camping trips and retreats. In areas where there are fewer homeschoolers or not as many organized activities, it may take a little more effort but it can be done. If quarterly school dances or parades are truly a high priority for your family, there is almost always a way to make them happen.

... And I'll Cry If I Want To

As we did earlier, it's important to look at the flip side of the coin. Not everyone had a magical experience at prom. Not everyone had a group or date with whom to go. For a variety of reasons, some kids felt that school dances were akin to torture. Whole groups of students in our high school chose to skip it and do their own thing. It's no different for many other school events. Some people love the atmosphere of rooting their team on at the homecoming game, but many couldn't care less about football and would rather be doing almost anything else. Tara, who blogs at *Embark on the Journey*,[20] shares the story of her two sons. One son was homeschooled and "didn't go to prom, but he could have if he wanted to … that just wasn't his thing." Her other son, attending public school, didn't attend a dance until his junior year; before that he "had the opportunity but not the desire."

In the movie *Office Space*,[21] one of the company bosses says to the main character, Peter Gibbons, "Looks like you've been missing a lot of work lately." Peter wryly replies, "Well, I wouldn't exactly say I've been 'missing' it, Bob." When homeschool fault-finders claim that homeschool group events are inadequate or nonexistent, one of the underlying assumptions is that all people find all of these events to be equally valuable, which simply isn't true.

Many kids really enjoy the school events but some, like myself, attend mainly because that's where their friends are. Dances were fun but, to be honest, I had just as much fun the times my friends and I skipped dances and went to play laser tag or to a nice dinner and sleepover party instead. With shiny new driver's licenses in our pockets, it felt exhilarating to plan and execute our own fun, experiencing the great big world on our own terms. Still other students, like Tara's son, just don't have the desire to attend certain events despite having the opportunity. If asked, they might tell you, "I wouldn't exactly say I've been 'missing' them, Bob."

Where There's a Will

So what happens if you *do* care about these social events, if your family *would* be missing them, but you still want to homeschool? First, take a close look at the desire or need being fulfilled by the event(s). For example, what is it about the homecoming football game that is exciting to you? Is it the sport itself? Is it just something to do?

20. "Do Homeschoolers Miss Out?," Embark on the Journey, accessed January 15, 2021, https://embarkonthejourney.com/do-homeschoolers-miss-out/.

21. *Office Space*, directed by Mike Judge (Los Angeles, CA: 20th Century Fox Home Entertainment, 1999), DVD.

Would you be just as happy eating s'mores at a backyard bonfire with the same friends? For some, it's the atmosphere of the game—the sounds of the band, the bright lights, the overpriced hot dogs, and the thrill of cheering on your team. Or is it the sense of belonging you have when surrounded by friends and peers gathered together in a common bond?

Once you've determined your true motivation, you can begin to brainstorm opportunities. Consider your specific situation. Many homeschoolers have public-schooled friends from the neighborhood with whom they can attend school functions. School football games are generally open to the community anyway, so grab a group of friends and get your cheer on! Or would attending a minor or major league baseball game with your homeschool group satisfy the same need for bonding over athletics? How about hosting weekly NFL parties during the season?

There are many opportunities available for other types of events as well. Community holiday parades, for example, are held annually in most areas. And high school homecoming parades and similar celebrations are usually open to anyone who wants to watch. Our homeschool marching band marches in several parades throughout the summer, so we've created new traditions around those events. Frankly, my younger kids don't much care what the parade is for, as long as there's someone there throwing candy their direction.

Many schools allow dances to be attended by non-students if they are accompanied by friends or dates from that school. For those not dating their public-schooled neighbor, other community dance opportunities are often available. In our mid-teens to early twenties, my friends and I loved taking the train to downtown Chicago to enjoy their regularly scheduled free dance lessons in Grant Park, which were followed by live music and dancing under the stars. Many towns, park districts, private groups, and even libraries host music festivals and dance events open to the public. Any of these could (and do) provide a chance for homeschooled kids to dress up and dance the night away.

Graduations, too, are special events that many homeschoolers don't want to miss. In our early days homeschooling, this was an area of concern for me personally as I didn't see a way to recreate for my kids the experience I had had at my high school graduation. Mine was a relatively large high school, so our graduation ceremony had many thousands of people in attendance. The sea of blue caps and gowns and an auditorium filled with family and faculty recognizing our years of hard work was quite a picture. It seemed almost cruel to me to not recognize my children's hard work and achievements, but there was just no way, as I saw it then, to recreate this experience with a graduating class of one.

But is that what our goal is here? To recreate the parents' memories and experiences? And is it the scale of the event that makes it special or important? If so, what does that mean for my public-schooled friend with the rural graduating class of forty-two students? If the number of attendees can make or break a graduation ceremony, what is the cutoff for a "valid" ceremony? A class of ten? Fifty? Two hundred? Obviously, there is no such magic number; yet, I still found myself questioning how my kids would have a "real" graduation experience.

Again (and this could be a motto for most homeschoolers) where there's a will, there's a way. Many statewide groups, such as the Home Educators Association of Virginia, for example, do host large-scale commencement events for homeschoolers. More locally, co-ops often host regular art and talent shows to showcase student work and have yearly graduation ceremonies for eighth graders and high schoolers. If yours doesn't, there's no time like the present to start one or more of these commemorative events.

Some families or groups hold portfolio exhibitions or graduation parties with relatives and friends. Apart from my mental picture of the sea of blue caps and gowns, I remember more from the post-graduation party hosted by my parents in our home than I do of the school's ceremony itself. The ocean of strangers' families might make it seem more spectacular at first glance, but ultimately it's the loving support and congratulations from those dearest to you and the student's own sense of accomplishment that matter most at a graduation.

5

Opportunity for Learning

We've talked, so far, about opportunities in terms of interaction with other people in general and in an extracurricular context. But what about the educational opportunities homeschoolers miss out on during the school day itself?

Since technology has made the academic content in most classes ubiquitous, it's become easier to see how parents really can access the materials they need to educate their kids. With just a few clicks, high-quality curricula can be shipped to your front porch. Both local and virtual solutions for individual learning, for every subject and at every age, are available to most families. But there are some things that can't be learned solo or taught without special equipment. In my experience, there are two school subjects most frequently brought up as areas of concern.

The first of these is gym class. More specifically, the experience of group games in P.E. or recess are thought to be lacking in home-based settings. After all, Duck Duck Goose is pretty pathetic with just two kids and a mom (trust me, I've tried). Red Rover, kickball, and flag football are just some of the many games that simply don't work unless you have a big group.

The other subject is science class. High school and even elementary science labs are equipped with all kinds of specialized equipment and safety gear. Most families don't have the budget to purchase the equipment needed for teaching units on organic chemistry or biology, let alone the dozens of other topics that each need different tools and materials.

It just seems difficult to imagine how homeschooled kids could be given opportunities in these problematic subjects, even if their mom did have enough energy to play baseball with them and clean up baking-soda-and-vinegar volcanoes every day (which I, for one, do not).

Goal!

Your response to this concern will be different depending on your location and individual circumstances. It will also vary greatly based on your objectives. For example, what *is* gym class? Why do we have it? Definitions vary, but my dictionary says that physical education is "instruction in the development and care of the body ranging from simple calisthenic exercises to a course of study providing training in hygiene, gymnastics, and the performance and management of athletic games."[22] Most of us would agree that traditional P.E. classes provide several benefits to students, including exercise, education in the rules and skill sets of various sports, practice in sportsmanship, and a "brain break" after which they can focus more effectively on other work.

Some options for the homeschooled student's gym class might look a lot like a traditional P.E. class. In fact, one option for some home-educated students *is* their public school gym class. For others, a co-op meeting once or a few times a week might provide a P.E. class comparable to any other school's class, complete with certified gym teacher or dedicated, sports-loving parent. To supplement a co-op gym class, some park districts or community centers offer homeschool open gym or similar programs. Local parks, pools, fitness centers, and group fitness classes, not to mention home gyms, trampolines, and swing sets, provide ample opportunity for exercise both in group settings and individually. Once we understand what

22. Frederick C. Mish, *Merriam-Webster's Collegiate Dictionary*, 10th ed. (Springfield, MA: Merriam-Webster, Inc., 1997).

the goals of a gym class are, it's not too hard to start thinking of countless ways to reach those objectives.

Consider a fictional homeschooled student—we'll call her Jamie—who has loved gymnastics since she first saw the sport in the Olympics on TV. Jamie's parents fostered this interest by enrolling her in a local private team where she's excelled and met a number of close friends. She's a supportive teammate and recently won their group's Team Spirit Award for excellent sportsmanship. Jamie also participates in a weekly co-op gym class where she's learned the basics of basketball, softball, dodgeball, flag football, and a number of other group games and common sports. On days with no gym class, gymnastics practice, or meets, she likes to jog around the neighborhood with her dog. Jamie's physical education program is a bit different than that of a public-schooled student. But does different mean that it's subpar? Obviously not. Here is a student who has found a unique way to meet the aforementioned goals of exercise, game play, sportsmanship, and healthy breaks while learning more about her own abilities and building important character traits and friendships along the way.

A Personalized Plan

One of the main benefits of homeschooling is the freedom to tailor education to your family's unique needs. What are the aims of your homeschool when it comes to physical education? Start listing your family's gym-related strengths and limitations as you think it through. Maybe your kids are already great team players and are getting plenty of exercise through their scouting hikes and volleyball team practices, but they need more exercise breaks during their school day. Maybe their dad is a huge sports fan and they've known the rules of football and baseball since he started their prenatal spring training, but they've also inherited his quick temper and poor sportsmanship. After taking an honest look at your circumstances, you can begin to find specific solutions to address your areas of concern and progress towards your goals.

For my own family, this exercise (pun intended) helped us determine how to approach our weekly P.E. routine. A one-hour co-op gym class was great for Mondays, but it simply wasn't enough. That class alone might not have been sufficient to meet our state's homeschool requirements, and I guarantee it wouldn't have been enough of an outlet for our active boys. So we supplemented with other classes and activities: gymnastics, swimming lessons, youth group games, bowling outings, and local sports leagues, to name a few. For years, we've also been attending a weekly indoor Homeschool Open Gym class where homeschooled kids are free to run and play together all afternoon.

Extended energetic playtimes with siblings and friends during traditional school hours—in combination with active learning moments peppered throughout most days (hopping down steps while practicing multiplication facts, for example)—provide ample opportunity for daily physical activity. Homeschooling parents encourage healthy, active lifestyles by blending all of these options to create balanced, personalized fitness plans for their children.

Sporty Spice

Another common worry is that homeschooling families don't have the equipment or know-how to teach various sports. Before we address that, first consider that "according to the *World Sports Encyclopedia* (2003), there are 8,000 indigenous sports and sporting games."[23] Obviously we'll need to trim down that list. But as we start removing less well-known sports, like ferret legging[24] and toe wrestling,[25] and whittle our list down to the more common fifty to one hundred choices, it becomes apparent that *any* physical education curriculum (like curricula for any subject) will still have inevitable gaps. Which sports are the critical ones for everyone to know? How well do they need to know them to succeed in life? Despite my at-

---

23. "List of Sports," Wikipedia, last modified January 14, 2021, https://en.wikipedia.org/wiki/List_of_sports.

24. "Ferret Legging," Wikipedia, last modified January 13, 2021, https://en.wikipedia.org/wiki/Ferret-legging.

25. "Toe wrestling," Wikipedia, last modified December 20, 2020, https://en.wikipedia.org/wiki/Toe_wrestling.

tending a well-regarded, well-funded high school with a thorough P.E. scope, I graduated not knowing how to play lacrosse or even what the game's equipment looks like. Some might say "so what?" to that, while others see it as a serious gap in my athletic education. For me, it hasn't mattered one bit.

So, is it possible that a family who can't afford lacrosse equipment could focus on the sports for which they already own equipment and still provide an acceptable gym experience for their kids? Of course! Start with what you have and go from there. Addressing perceived weaknesses like this is often easier than you might think once you start brainstorming assets that may have been overlooked. You may only have basic sports equipment like bikes, a basketball, and a soccer ball, but that's a great start. Even those who truly have next to nothing are able to fashion equipment to play games.

My son's Awana (church youth group) handbook describes how some kids in Nepal make their own youth group game supplies such as using bamboo sticks in lieu of relay race batons.[26] Necessity is the mother of invention, as the old proverb goes. But even without necessity's motivation, kids are naturally creative and inventive, especially when they have a goal (another sports pun, sorry) in mind. My own kids once had a blast making a kickball out of plastic bags and a string and used it for months instead of the variety of "real" equipment in our garage. Running barefoot, Abebe Bikila won the gold in the marathon at the 1960 Summer Olympics.[27] As a child, Pelé, one of the most famous soccer players of all time, practiced with a rag-stuffed sock because his family couldn't afford a soccer ball.[28] Fancy equipment is nice, but clearly not necessary for success; it's the icing on the cake.

I say these things to help us keep this in perspective. But be assured that home-educating families have numerous options when it

---

26. Awana, *Awana Sparks WingRunner Handbook 2* (Streamwood, IL: Awana Clubs International, 2013), 53.

27. "Abebe Bikila," Wikipedia, last modified January 5, 2021, https://en.wikipedia.org/wiki/Abebe_Bikila.

28. "Pelé," Encyclopedia.com, accessed January 15, 2021, https://www.encyclopedia.com/people/sports-and-games/sports-biographies/pele-soccer-player.

comes to obtaining equipment if needed and desired. Family, friends, and neighbors are great sources for borrowing equipment for a unit study on a specific sport. Co-ops, churches, or community sports centers might have a lending library for equipment or allow you to use it upon request with a court or field reservation. If several families coordinate efforts, they can share the costs of field rentals and specialized equipment. After politely requesting access to a wider selection of equipment for our local Homeschool Open Gym class, our park district not only opened their storage closets for us but also generously purchased new equipment specifically for our group. They were more than happy to help—all we needed to do was ask.

More often than not, if you've found someone who has the equipment you need, you've probably also found someone who would love to teach you all they know about the game. One doesn't need worksheets and quizzes to learn the rules of a sport. Think of the different perspectives and information your child could amass by interviewing the owner of your local bowling alley and sitting in on a few league games with bowlers who have been playing for twenty years. An outing to the bowling alley, a field trip to a professional hockey game, a Sunday night football game on TV, or a summer pool pass—all of these are opportunities to learn the ins and outs of various sports. We just need to be intentional about making the most of them.

From family to local community to the internet, gym class content and opportunities are everywhere. Remember, for all parents, regardless of your family's educational style, your own attitudes towards exercise will likely be more influential than whatever they learned in their co-op or public school P.E. class. So take a look at your own habits and the behaviors you're modeling. Then think about your goals, budget, assets, and limitations and begin imagining what your family's unique gym class experience might look like. The sky is the limit, so think creatively. Sporty spice it up!

Home Sweet Laboratory

Gym class is one thing; science, however, seems like an even more critical issue to many parents. How can a homeschooling family provide their kids the opportunity for quality science learning when they don't have the equipment, know-how, or physical space? How do home educators tackle this academic subject? I, too, wondered all of this early in our homeschooling journey.

Several of the projects I worked on as an architectural intern early in my career were laboratory facilities for companies like Hospira (now part of Pfizer) and Abbott Laboratories. To say that the design stipulations and building code requirements for facilities like these are detailed and comprehensive would be an understatement. Due to the nature of work done in these labs, there are exceedingly specific requirements for almost every aspect of the design, from HEPA air filtration systems and airlocks to specialized biocontainment precautions for each of four biosafety levels (BSLs).

In the United States, labs processing biological agents are designated BSL-1 (the lowest level) to BSL-4 (the highest level requiring the most precautions). Most high school laboratories are BSL-1. Upon learning this, some prospective homeschoolers might wonder which corner of their basement they'll need to fix up to meet the BSL-1 requirements so they can teach their sophomore chemistry. Okay, I'm probably the only one who actually wondered that. But, in all seriousness, it was a significant worry for me that I might not be able to provide an adequate science foundation for my kids.

In actuality, though, I've found it's not too hard to do. By taking more than just a cursory glance at the issues, we can almost always get to a workable solution. The best approach is to get specific within the context of your unique circumstances. Avoid making sweeping generalizations (as I did when first starting out) such as "I don't have a lab, so I can't do science." Just as you did for gym class, consider what equipment you *do* have available and what, specifically, you'd need to find elsewhere.

Maybe your dad, like mine, owns a telescope and is willing to lend it out for your astronomy unit. Maybe your teen son loves biology and a high-quality microscope is within reach if you split the cost of one with him. Or perhaps you found the same YouTube video[29] I did and turned your iPhone into a basic microscope with a handful of inexpensive parts (I was skeptical, but amazingly it worked). Do you think you have access to a local community college's lab? If not, are you sure? Have you asked? Is there a homeschool resource center near you that lends out equipment? Just like with sports, look around for local companies, schools, or community facilities that might have what you need. Don't assume. Ask.

Science Is Everywhere

If the first step in my educational worldview shift was realizing that socialization was possible for homeschoolers, the second was the epiphany I had when I understood that the homeschooling parent doesn't have to *know* everything or *teach* everything or *own* everything. I can assure you there will be no dissected frog carcasses or

— ...

The homeschooling parent doesn't have to know *everything or* teach *everything or* own *everything.*

— ...

sheep brains in my kitchen (although there are many resources[30] available for those who aren't as squeamish as I am). Nevertheless, my kids have had and will continue to have plenty of opportunities to participate in dissections and other laboratory projects throughout their science education.

There are online courses specifically geared towards homeschoolers, real-time and on-demand virtual lab classes, plus local co-ops

---

29. Kenji Yoshino, "Turn Your Smartphone into a Digital Microscope!," uploaded to YouTube October 16, 2013, https://www.youtube.com/watch?v=KpMTkr_aiYU.

30. For lab supplies and science equipment, try online suppliers like Carolina Biological Supply Company (https://www.carolina.com).

(like ours) and academies that provide in-person labs and high school–level courses. The natural flexibility in scheduling that comes with the homeschooling lifestyle also allows students to pursue lab-based dual-credit options, special interest or STE(A)M homeschool camps, and internships and apprenticeships outside of their home that might not otherwise be possible.

Keep in mind that science is the study of the natural, created universe. Literally everything you see (plus tiny matter and energy invisible to the naked eye) falls under the umbrella of "science." Don't let sterile school labs with their Bunsen burners and fifteen matching microscopes intimidate you. You *can* lead your kids through scientific investigations on your own or with the guidance of a quality curriculum, of which there are many. And, if you just can't imagine implementing science in your home in any way, that still doesn't mean you can't homeschool. It simply means that science will be a subject you outsource.

The "Right" Stuff

Starting out, I thought my biggest challenge would be finding ways to duplicate the ambiguous "range of options" King described. I just didn't see how we could recreate it all on our own at home. To the contrary, I now find that one of my biggest challenges is sifting through *too many* opportunities! We're absolutely inundated with possibilities for socialization, academic enrichment in all subjects, and even access to specialized equipment and facilities. There is *so* much available. Remember, though, no public school, private school, or homeschool has it all, whatever "all" means.

The opportunities afforded by the public school down the street will differ from those available at your local private schools. Further, public schools in different states or towns (to say nothing of other countries) can have vastly different opportunities than other public schools even when following the same content standards. Our homeschool provides opportunities tailored to our family, which will invariably look different than the "range of options" offered by our homeschooling friends' families. Socializing with friends over lunch, attending dances and graduations, learning to play tennis, or stargazing through a telescope are all opportunities available for the taking if they are important or necessary for your child or your family.

To say that there's one "right" set of possibilities, or to suggest that the particular range of options available within one system of educating is what *every* student should be aiming for, is unnecessarily limiting. Opportunities utterly abound if we look for them. I know it can be hard to think of other ways of doing things when most of us have only known one way. It just takes a willingness to think outside the box—and not even very far outside the box. Just open it slightly and peek out, and you'll be surprised at the ideas that start coming to you.

In order to think about opportunity, first start by defining your terms and letting go of preconceptions. Talk with your family about your unique needs and circumstances and brainstorm ways to satisfy those needs within the constraints of your situation. As businessman and writer Jacob Gelt Dekker so wisely reminds us, "Opportunities are always everywhere, learn to see and create them."[31]

---

31. "Jacob Gelt Dekker quotes," AZquotes website, accessed January 15, 2021, https://www.azquotes.com/author/28691-Jacob_Gelt_Dekker.

6

Effectiveness of the Home Educator

Hopefully you now agree, or already knew, that opportunity is far from lacking in a home education. Maybe the question in your mind is not *quantitative* but *qualitative*. That is, opportunities for relationships, activities, and learning in home education may be numerous, but are they high caliber? Are they any good? Parents might be present more, but are they effective teachers? Curricula, classes, and co-ops may be plentiful, but are homeschooled kids actually learning anything? Is a home-based education really a high-*quality* option?

First Things First

Just as we did when looking at socialization, let's begin by defining (or at least narrowing down the scope of) the term "effective." For a method of education to be deemed "effective" it needs to produce or bring about a desired effect. Based on this definition, any dialogue about a system's effectiveness when compared to another presupposes an agreed-upon "desired effect."[32] So, for the sake of general discussion, let's use a paraphrased version of Wikipedia's paragraph

32. "Definition of Effective," Merriam-Webster, Inc., accessed January 16, 2021, https://www.merriam-webster.com/dictionary/effective.

on the purpose of education. An effective or successful education encompasses a combination of personal and community factors. It will positively influence students' personal development (in terms of autonomy, identity, and career) and promote good citizenship which, in turn, positively impacts our society.[33]

Many individuals and groups have undertaken to research and understand the innumerable aspects that make up the parts and whole of an effective education. Evidence-based recommendations are plentiful, guiding educators towards touted successful strategies and best practices at all levels.

There are some groups focused on very specific facets of education. For example, the Handedness Research Institute "advances the scientific understanding of handedness … and helps alleviate the social and educational discrimination of left-handers worldwide through research and education."[34] Some corporations, such as the aptly named Institute for Effective Education, focus on the "principles and methods established by behavioral science research" to improve operations at the individual school and curricular level.[35] Having an even more extensive reach are measures such as the Common Core State Standards Initiative which "establish[es] clear, consistent guidelines for what every student should know and be able to do in math and English language arts from kindergarten through 12th grade"[36] and which impacts schools across the country.

Even if we can tentatively agree on a definition of effectiveness, clearly the scope of this topic is overwhelming. Every aspect of education—from a preschooler's pencil grip to a high school's elective course offerings—has been researched and overanalyzed by experts somewhere. Even if they could agree on the "right answers" in all of this research (which is far from being the case), it would be impos-

---

33. "Education," Wikipedia, section: "Theory"; subsection: "Purpose," last modified January 11, 2021, https://en.wikipedia.org/wiki/Education.

34. Handedness Research Institute (website), accessed January 16, 2021, http://handedness.org/.

35. "Mission Statement," The Institute for Effective Education, accessed January 16, 2021, https://www.tiee.org/about/mission-statement/.

36. "What Parents Should Know," Common Core State Standards Initiative, accessed January 16, 2021, http://www.corestandards.org/what-parents-should-know/.

sible for one educator or one school, regardless of type, to implement all facets of the elusive "most effective education."

So, to rein in what otherwise could be a never-ending chapter, our discussion of the efficacy of homeschooling will focus on three of the most common areas of doubt: unlicensed/uncertified teachers teaching (i.e., homeschooling parents, most often moms), students not learning the right material in the right way, and young home-schooled adults being ill prepared for adulthood.

The Professional Homeschool Parent

For me, the thought of standing in front of a group of twenty thir-teen-year-olds is terrifying, especially if only a few are interested in what I'm saying and there's a time limit and a test on Friday. Before we embarked on our homeschooling journey, and with only my own background as a public-schooled student from which to draw, I simply couldn't imagine myself stepping into the role of "teacher." I had essen-tially zero teacher training and no relevant degree or certification, so I recall thinking that I must be either very naive or very arrogant to even entertain the idea. The handful of times in my life when I've been the instructor in a classroom setting were enough to demonstrate that my gifts and inclinations lie elsewhere. One vivid example comes to mind.

As I said earlier, my background is in architecture and architec-tural engineering. For those unfamiliar with the industry, the last few decades have seen a rise in environmentally friendly building design and materials. Besides meeting code-required sustainability goals, there are several optional "green" certification programs that recog-nize particularly healthy, environmentally friendly buildings. One of the most popular of these programs is LEED (Leadership in Energy and Environmental Design) certification, which "is a globally rec-ognized symbol of sustainability achievement."[37] Normally, my job descriptions never included "teaching a class." But, years ago, as the guinea pig in my architecture office who obtained their LEED-AP

---

37. "LEED Rating System," U.S. Green Building Council, accessed January 16, 2021, https://www.usgbc.org/leed.

(LEED Accredited Professional)[38] credential first, I was subsequently given the opportunity to teach LEED exam prep classes for coworkers and other business owners outside of my own office.

Although all of my students did pass their LEED exams, it was likely in spite of my classroom teaching abilities, not because of them. I can only imagine what it was like for the listeners as they tried to follow me along rabbit trails which were more akin to free associations in a therapy session than the topics in our class notes. Thankfully, there were PowerPoint printouts they could take home for their own study. As for behavior management, my efforts at settling the group down so we could focus on our work were futile. Even as adults, there were class clowns over whom I held no sway.

—————————————————— · · ·

"Homeschool parent" and "classroom teacher" are not the same thing.

—————————————————— · · ·

"How can this be?" you may ask. Isn't a homeschool teacher who can't teach a class an oxymoron? This leads us to another of the most misunderstood elements of homeschooling. "Homeschool parent" and "classroom teacher" are *not* the same thing. The profession of homeschooling parent is its own distinct (and unfortunately unpaid) occupation. Although there is certainly some overlap with other professions when it comes to helpful skill sets and areas of expertise, the role of homeschool mom or dad is unique and highly customizable. While it's true that I'd likely be ineffective teaching a room of twenty junior high school students, I've found that simply has no bearing on my ability to teach and guide my own children, or even small groups of homeschooled kids at our co-op, in completely different settings.

---

38. A LEED-AP is a person who has passed the LEED-AP exam of their specialty which "measure[s] knowledge about green building, a specific LEED rating system and the certification process." Accessed January 16, 2021, https://www.usgbc.org/credentials/leed-ap.

Some homeschooling parents are or were traditional school-teachers, and some with teaching ability do teach their children in the more traditional sense of the term. Many of them also utilize their classroom teaching skills to help the larger homeschool community. But neither a teaching degree nor even teaching experience is a prerequisite for successful homeschooling. It's not uncommon for teachers-turned-homeschooling-parents to report[39] that their teaching experience is actually of limited help to them (or is even a hindrance) in their home educating because it's hard to break out of the methodologies that have been ingrained in them. They try unsuccessfully to recreate the public school experience in their homes and eventually realize that they need to set aside practices that were created for a different setting to take full advantage of the benefits of homeschooling.

Once we start to unpack the differences between the role of a traditional classroom teacher and the role of a homeschooling parent, the concern about homeschools being instructed by "unlicensed teachers" becomes a moot point. It's a little bit like comparing the truck driver for a nationwide grocery store to a woman who delivers homegrown organic fruit to her neighbors on her bicycle. They are both transporting produce, but clearly they are not the same jobs.

Apples and Oranges

If homeschooling parents teach but aren't exactly teachers, then what are we? It may be easiest to approach this question from the opposite perspective. What parts of the traditional teacher role are we *not*? Jeanne Faulconer, blogger at *TheHomeschoolMom.com*, offers a good starting point in her "Ask Jeanne" column, where she addresses frequently asked questions about homeschooling. When a mom with a background in teaching elementary school posted a question about transitioning to her new role as homeschooling mom, Jeanne advised her to "think about how much you did in a classroom was be-

---

39. For example, see http://worshipfulliving.com/2016/05/09/confessions-of-a-teacher-turned-home-school-mom/.

cause you were in a classroom—with 25 kids who had to get through a set curriculum."[40]

All the knowledge of standards, testing, required curriculum, and lesson planning aren't necessary for homeschoolers. All the red tape, forms, memos, communication with principals, committees, and parent–teacher conferences usually don't apply. The practical skills in classroom management, grading methods, and public speaking—all of those skills that are typically so integral and important to the job of a classroom teacher—are, to some degree or another, *optional* in homeschooling. Even in states where certain standards must be followed or certain tests given, the homeschooling parent's day-to-day job description doesn't necessarily need to look like that of a public or private school teacher and is often far from it.

Consider our previous produce delivery analogy. The commercial produce truck driver—let's call him Ed—is providing a necessary and important service, delivering hundreds of cases of fruits and vegetables in each of his daily runs. Due to the scale of his impact and the nature of the commercial business system in which he works, certain regulations and compulsory protocols must be followed to ensure safe, timely, and efficient fruit delivery. The red tape is annoying at times, but it's a necessary tradeoff so that thousands of families can benefit from his efforts.

Ed's position requires him to attend continuing education classes on various topics such as efficient truck packing, gas-saving driving strategies, and improving interactions between drivers and grocery store owners. Of course, he also keeps up with his commercial driver's license (CDL) renewal fees and associated vision and written tests. His ability to consistently pack his truck efficiently and safely, meet his required deadlines, and skillfully communicate with bosses, store owners, and coworkers alike make him an ideal worker. In fact, Ed's boss has given Ed the opportunity to train and mentor other

---

40. Jeanne Faulconer, "Ask Jeanne: When a Teacher Turns Homeschool Mom," The Homeschool Mom, accessed January 16, 2021, https://www.thehomeschoolmom.com/ask-jeanne-teacher-turns-homeschool-mom/.

new hires due to his experience and engaging personality. It is fair to say that Ed is an effective produce deliverer.

Now meet Lucy, a retired woman who loves gardening and maintains a variety of fruit trees in her back yard. She started giving her excess produce to her friends and neighbors and recently bought a bicycle and small bike trailer so she could deliver more efficiently. She has made it her policy to deliver fruit the day she picks it and always sets aside the largest apples for Mr. Jones and the ripest pears for Mrs. Smith to suit their individual preferences. Lately, in her spare time, Lucy has been researching maintenance tips for her new bike trailer and improved pruning methods to increase her trees' yields.

Lucy has been a member of her local garden club for years, trading ideas, tips, and harvest samples with other enthusiasts on a biweekly basis. She's led a few discussion groups and seminars at her local library for beginning gardeners. She is well regarded by her peers as a wealth of information on backyard gardening and is loved and appreciated by her friends and neighbors. Lucy, like Ed, is an effective produce deliverer.

• • •

The homeschooling parent is essentially a tutor whose specialty is facilitating and guiding the learning of their own child(ren).

• • •

Ed and Lucy are similar in some ways. At the end of the day, their most basic goal is the same: they both want to have delivered produce to the best of their ability and to have used their gifts and talents to benefit others. But to try to force them into the same box—to require Ed to take classes in fruit tree pruning or make Lucy obtain a CDL—is nonsensical at best. They are simply related but different work. Not better, not worse. Just different.

Similarly, the role of homeschooling parent is related to the role of K–12 classroom teacher, but they are different professions. Neither is better or worse. Just different. In many ways, the role of a homeschooling parent is more closely aligned to the role of a tutor than of a teacher. The homeschooling parent is essentially a tutor whose specialty is facilitating and guiding the learning of their own child(ren). Just like many tutors and some private school teachers, homeschooling parents do not need a teaching certificate or license to do their jobs well. Relevant research[41] consistently shows that there is no statistically significant difference in student achievement (read: "effectiveness") when comparing homeschools led by parents with and without teaching certificates. A study in *Academic Leadership Live: The Online Journal* even found that "the [homeschooled] students having neither parent ever certified performed slightly *better*"[42] (emphasis added).

Of course, this in no way diminishes the accomplishment of those who have worked hard to obtain their teaching certificate. Recalling our produce analogy, to state that Lucy doesn't need a CDL to deliver produce on her bike in no way reduces the need for Ed to get one, nor does it devalue Ed's achievement in obtaining his CDL. Again, it's comparing apples and oranges. Homeschooling parents aren't driving trucks; they're riding bikes.

In light of all this, I find it more accurate to refer to homeschooling parents as home *educators* rather than homeschool *teachers*. Many professions fall under the broad umbrella term of "educator" and not all of them are required to have teaching certificates. All educators have in common the basic goal of educating those under their tutelage. Depending on the setting in which an educator works, though, the job description and skills required might be dramatically different. The assumption that education or certification requirements for various types of educators should be the same is errant and leads to all manner of unnecessary waste. Time, energy, and resources spent

---

41. For a summary of relevant research, see https://www.nheri.org/home-school-researcher-parent-education-levels-as-they-relate-to-academic-achievement-among-home-schooled-children/.

42. Brian D. Ray, "Academic Achievement and Demographic Traits of Homeschool Students: A Nationwide Study," *Academic Leadership* 8 no. 1 (Winter 2010): 20, https://www.nheri.org/wp-content/uploads/2018/03/Ray-2010-Academic-Achievement-and-Demographic-Traits-of-Homeschool-Students.pdf.

fulfilling irrelevant requirements would be better spent honing the skills needed to excel in their *own* unique setting.

In some cases, a standard credential is a beneficial tool. It can be helpful to confirm that an educator has a certain set of knowledge or level of expertise. Requiring credentials can also provide criteria for sifting through high volumes of job applicants. Other times, as is the case in some private schools and charter schools, previous work experience or degrees in your field are more valuable indicators of educator effectiveness. In a tutoring or homeschooling setting, the ability to tailor methods to the needs of individual students is critical to success; therefore, the quantity of time spent observing the student and developing the educator–student relationship might be a better predictor of effectiveness. For all educators, though, time in the trenches—time spent actually doing the job of educating their students, whatever the setting—will be the fastest way to improve their effectiveness.

Learn as You Go

Not only is the role of homeschooling parent not the same as a classroom teacher, but the skill sets utilized to homeschool effectively vary greatly from family to family. This is one of the reasons that homeschooling is successful in such a wide variety of families and situations. One outgoing mom I know, who loves themed parties, artistic expression, and hosting events, uses those same skills to prepare exciting themed lessons and host memorable hands-on art opportunities for the families in our co-op. A homeschooling dad, who is also a veteran, uses his military training and youthful energy to keep the kids in a local homeschool gym class engaged and on task. The parent who has lesson planning experience can create customized lessons for each child, while the parent with a penchant for reading and research can find the best resources and methods to fit her family's learning styles. Each educator's unique style will unfold out of their own strengths and passions. Their methods can be developed over time as they learn about themselves and their students and together work to create their ideal learning setting.

The concern about stepping into the role of homeschooling mom without any kind of teacher training was a roadblock—almost a deal breaker—for me personally. I recall being very skeptical when I first read or heard things along the lines of "parents only need to be literate and committed to the home school process"[43] or "if you love your kids and are motivated to help them learn, you can acquire the skills you need."[44] There simply *has* to be more to it than that, I thought. But the more I reflected on it, the more I realized that my entire adult life is a testament to the validity of these assertions. Necessary job skills *can* be picked up along the way with commitment, motivation, and a willingness to learn.

My college training was in architectural engineering with a specialty in construction management. If I had followed the traditional path for those with my educational background, either I'd be working at an engineering firm developing electrical, mechanical, or structural systems for buildings or I'd be on a job site managing construction projects for a commercial general contractor. It worked out, though, that my college summer internships were always at architecture firms despite my having taken almost no architectural design classes. The two fields—engineering and architecture—are related; knowing general building terminology and AutoCAD software certainly helped. But as I moved on from internships to full-time work, the vast majority of my architectural design and technical skills were developed on the job and through working world experience.

Or, consider another example. Like many other homeowners, my husband and I have successfully tackled numerous home renovations with minimal background in carpentry and we have a thriving vegetable garden without any horticultural degrees. I say this not to brag but to demonstrate that a regular Joe or Jane with a need or desire really *can* self-educate and achieve success in areas outside the scope of their "official training." We never did get our Bachelor of How to Be Married degrees or Certificates in Parenting, but, with much prayer and ongoing efforts towards improvement, we've been

---

43. Ray E. Ballmann, *The How and Why of Home Schooling* (Wheaton, IL: Crossway Books, 1995), 184.
44. Debra Bell, *The Ultimate Guide to Homeschooling* (Nashville, TN: Tommy Nelson, 2000), 51.

able to continually acquire the skills needed for these two areas of our lives through "on-the-job training" as well.

The book you're reading right now is another illustration of this point. I've enjoyed writing in various capacities in the past but I have no degree in writing, English, or literature. The authors of *Sparks of Genius* describe writer Kurt Vonnegut's thoughts about this when he argues that future fiction writers won't be found in English classes. "They will, he [Vonnegut] believes, be found in the sciences and medicine, for mastery of those crafts will provide not only the basis for writing great fiction but the unusual experiences needed to enrich it."[45] One's unique life experiences (whether in school or outside of it), in combination with God-given talents and sufficient motivation, can and do lead to success and achievement in all areas of humanity.

. . .

With a calling or desire and a commitment to the process, you really can acquire the skills needed to transition successfully into the role of homeschooling parent and effectively homeschool your child(ren).

. . .

By the time we finished our first year of homeschooling, I began to see how the veteran homeschool authors quoted earlier were right. With a calling or desire and a commitment to the process, you really *can* acquire the skills needed to transition successfully into the role of homeschooling parent and effectively homeschool your child(ren). That's not to say it's easy, and it definitely won't look the same for everyone. One of the main advantages of homeschooling is the freedom to individualize the experience, not just for the students but for the parents as well.

45. Robert Root-Bernstein and Michèle Root-Bernstein, *Sparks of Genius: The 13 Thinking Tools of the World's Most Creative People* (Boston, NY: Houghton Mifflin Company, 1999), 324.

With the ability to tailor their job description to their strengths and improve on or compensate for areas of weakness, truly the vast majority of parents motivated to homeschool can do so effectively. The proof is in the proverbial pudding. Research repeatedly demonstrates that "whether [or not] homeschool parents were ever certified teachers is *not* related to their children's academic achievement" (emphasis added). Beyond that, "homeschool students score above average on achievement tests regardless of their parents' formal level of education."[46] As you consider the possibility of homeschooling, please don't allow the myth that "you're not qualified" to become a stumbling block. It simply isn't true.

Why Parents Are Effective Teachers

Before we move on, it's worth mentioning here that effective (and ineffective) teaching can happen anywhere. When we begin making sweeping statements such as "homeschooling parents can't be effective because they aren't certified teachers" or "public school teachers can't be effective within the confines of a broken system," we do those educators and our families a disservice. We owe it to all involved, especially our kids, to take a closer look before we make such bold pronouncements of what is and isn't possible.

Consider reading instruction, for example. When discussing reading assignments in traditional schools in their book *The Case Against Homework*, authors Sara Bennett and Nancy Kalish give examples of tedious reading assignments that suck the joy out of literature. They quote numerous students whose experiences with certain books were ruined by inane homework requirements and monotonous worksheets assigned to them. Clearly ineffective. Yet the authors also share stories of incredibly talented teachers whose openended reading assignments inspire kids to love reading and generate valuable discussions. Bennett and Kalish believe that "if our goal is to raise literate children, we need to raise children who want to laze

---

46. Brian D. Ray, "Research Facts on Homeschooling," January 15, 2021, https://www.nheri.org/research-facts-on-homeschooling/.

around with a good book—a book that they can't put down because it's so fantastic."[47] Some of the teachers they interviewed were able to guide their students towards exactly this kind of appreciation for reading—the kind that will last a lifetime.

The same holds true in any industry. In my own previous line of work, there were architects who you could tell truly loved their profession. They'd read trade magazines in their free time, practice the latest drafting programs for fun, and consistently provide a high level of quality design to their clients, often going above and beyond what was expected. Then there were those for whom architecture was "just a job." They weren't necessarily "bad" architects; many did fine work and were friendly people. But they generally did just the minimum required and definitely wouldn't be found reading industry journals on their lunch break. Beyond that were the architects who, although employed and even licensed, had neither design ability nor business sense.

Think of your own career or your experiences with virtually any service provider whom you've encountered. There are plumbers you'd recommend to your neighbor and plumbers you'd recommend they avoid. There are effective salespeople who believe in their product and are working to improve people's lives, but there are also salespeople who just want to make a buck. I recall an experience with one dentist that left me thinking about a malpractice suit. On the other hand, I also remember having an orthodontist whose gentle bedside manner almost (*almost*) offset the torturous experience of having my braces tightened. Both the dentist and orthodontist had the proper credentials and private practices and yet their impact on me, their patient, couldn't have been more different.

No test can measure all of the intangible elements needed to teach a classroom full of kids or homeschool or do any job "effectively." Licenses and certificates generally *aren't even measures of effectiveness*. They are tools used to determine qualification for *beginning* your work in a given field. They really say nothing about your effectiveness in your day-to-day work. As someone blessed with the abil-

---

47. Sara Bennett and Nancy Kalish, *The Case Against Homework: How Homework Is Hurting Children and What Parents Can Do About It* (New York, NY: Three Rivers Press, 2007), 132.

ity to do well on tests, I can personally attest that a license, certificate, or even a degree doesn't necessarily guarantee genuine understanding of the relevant content.

Clearly there are effective and ineffective individuals in any field, but when it comes to education, the stakes are higher because the "clients" are vulnerable, impressionable children whose futures hang on the words and actions of those in charge. Books, media, and most people's personal experiences are replete with examples of students whose attitude towards learning, feelings about math (or any other subject), self esteem, career path, or belief in themselves was impacted, for better or worse, by a certain educator.

It's the richness—the trust, the family bond, the depth—of the relationship between the child and parent that is one of the most important keys to the effectiveness of a parent-educator.

In education, it's a person's love for their students, ability to help them grow as individuals, and desire to instill values and a love of learning that are keys to effectiveness. Parents are uniquely positioned to instill family values and model a love of learning and curiosity in a natural and consistent way for their children. And, of course, in most instances, no one is more motivated to see a child grow than his parents. After all, it's not his third-grade teacher's basement he'll be living in when he's forty if he failed to mature or get a job.

Joking aside, it's the richness—the trust, the family bond, the depth—of the relationship between the child and parent that is one of the most important keys to the effectiveness of a parent-educator. Home educators are effective not because of a certain license or piece of paper but because they can handcraft and implement an individualized educational plan for each of their unique children within the context of a love for each child that is unmatched.

7

Effectiveness of the Process

Consider these summary statements from multiple sources of data:

"The home-educated typically score 15 to 30 percentile points above public-school students on standardized academic achievement tests."

"Home-educated students typically score above average on the SAT and ACT tests that colleges consider for admissions. … Homeschool students are increasingly being actively recruited by colleges."

"[Homeschooling] may be the fastest-growing form of education in the United States. Home-based education has also been growing around the world in many other nations (e.g., Australia, Canada, France, Hungary, Japan, Kenya, Russia, Mexico, South Korea, Thailand, and the United Kingdom)."[48]

And yet, despite clear statistics that homeschooling is effective and that it's increasingly becoming more popular, it's still hard to imagine how this grassroots, homespun, DIY education really works.

---

48. Brian D. Ray, "Research Facts on Homeschooling," January 15, 2021, https://www.nheri.org/research-facts-on-homeschooling/.

The public school procedures and practices that most of us experienced are deeply ingrained and can be very difficult to shake. It's simply hard to conceive of doing things a different way, and it's difficult to understand how another way could work as well as, or better than, "the usual way."

Non-homeschoolers, or those new to the scene, often hear (or assume) things about homeschooling that just don't seem to make sense. No assigned grade levels? No grading or regular standardized testing? Mom picking curricula from random sources she found online? Different scopes and sequences of educational materials? Won't there be gaps in the students' knowledge? How will you have any idea what to teach next or who's learned what? To put it bluntly, it sounds like sheer chaos to some.

———————————————————— · · ·

There is no single best, right method.

———————————————————— · · ·

To address these issues, we have to think about the framework in which most of us have grown up and been educated. Ultimately, all of these questions are asking how home educators can be certain they're teaching the right material in the right way and at the right time. This is predicated on the thinking that there *is* a "right" way and a "right" time to learn the "right" content. As a recovering perfectionist, and someone overly focused on efficiency, I've wrestled often with the idea of finding the "right" or "best" way in many areas of life, and homeschooling has been no exception.

The more I conducted my own educational research and the deeper we dove into the homeschooling lifestyle, the more my thinking began to change. Searching for the "one right, best way" to educate all children is futile; each person is unique and the situations they are being trained in and for are also diverse. Therefore, *there is no single best, right method.* This is why highly customizable options such as home education, apprenticeships, private tutoring, and the like have stood the test of time; their efficacy has been proven successful over millennia. As we'll see next, both historical and modern educational experiences and research continually, and often unknowingly, point in the direction of homeschooling as a high-quality method of educating children.

Homeschools Can Do That

Mitsuo Ogata, a Japanese mathematician, philosopher, and author describes his own transformative journey towards true, lifelong, curiosity-driven learning in his book, *We Could All Become Geniuses*. As a young student, learning new ideas was difficult for him, as was creative thinking. As he puts it, he "used to constantly struggle with learning and thinking."[49] After an IQ test confirmed that he was only "average," he felt a tremendous amount of frustration and self-doubt. Over time, though, he was able to break free from the labels and traditional learning conventions. He trained his brain to observe his surroundings, ask effective questions, and recapture the excitement of learning. He observes that "challenging the dogma of established teaching methods has produced tremendous results beyond [his] expectation."[50]

Homeschoolers have the freedom to "challenge the dogma" and to approach learning in new and individualized ways. Ogata goes on to describe other benefits to nontraditional, self-led learning. Many of the ideas he mentions are commonplace in homeschools. "Leveraging the momentum of curiosity, fresh memory, and high interest does seem to make it so much easier to learn because it is so much easier to think."[51] As I read Ogata's book, I found myself nodding in agreement to quotes like this and thinking that's why homeschooling is so effective for so many families. In fact, I began to notice in many education books I was reading that—whenever authors or researchers were driving home their main ideas about successful learning techniques, improving retention, inspiring a love of learning,

---

49. Mitsuo Ogata, *We Could All Become Geniuses: Seeking Fun in Learning and Thinking* (Barrington Hills, IL: Duke Ogata, 2013), 1.

50. Ogata, *Geniuses*, 55.

51. Ogata, *Geniuses*, 58.

and increasing educational effectiveness—I found myself thinking, "They're describing homeschools! Homeschooling already does that!"

Even education-related literature that doesn't directly mention homeschooling or self-led learning often points us to homeschooling as an effective educational method and demonstrates that there is no such thing as the "right" content, time, or methodology for all children in all situations. The following brief literature review uses a small handful of examples from a variety of *non*-homeschool-related sources to demonstrate this point.

The "Right" Content

In his book *The Quality School: Managing Students Without Coercion*, William Glasser, MD writes "the most obvious measure of the effective teachers we remember is that they were not boring; somehow or other what they asked us to do was satisfying to us."[52] Many homeschoolers, especially those who follow an unschooling or child-led-learning approach, would tell you this is one of their main daily objectives. What is satisfying or interesting to one person might not be relevant or interesting to another; hence, the ability to tailor the scope and sequence of study is critical to effectiveness. Homeschools have more freedom than any other method of education to do this well.

Leonardo da Vinci stated the same basic truth long ago when he observed that "study without desire spoils the memory, and it retains nothing that it takes in."[53] Rather than forcing a set of knowledge onto students because a certain standard, curriculum, or test requires it, homeschooling provides the space and time needed to cultivate true learning about topics of interest that are relevant and necessary for each student. In *Learning & Memory: The Brain in Action*, Marilee Sprenger states the same thing in another way when she writes "cramming is how many of us got through school. It is effec-

---

52. William Glasser, *The Quality School: Managing Students without Coercion* (New York, NY: HarperPerennial, 1998), 8.

53. "Leonardo da Vinci Quotes," GoodReads, accessed January 16, 2021, https://www.goodreads.com/quotes/53112-study-without-desire-spoils-the-memory-and-it-retains-nothing.

tive for the moment, but it does not provide meaningful information that remains in the brain as neural networks to which connections can be added."[54]

Instead, homeschooling encourages the student to take ownership of their education and facilitates the "meaningful student involvement" extolled as the key to success in mainstream education literature. For example, in a home education setting, it's easy to "[engage] students as partners in every facet of school change for the purpose of strengthening their commitment to education, community, and democracy."[55] It allows them to "focus on cultivating [their] own skills and passions" instead of "competing for the same standard résumé builders as everyone else."[56] This leads to long-term retention of content but also satisfaction with the learning process and their education. "Children who spend oodles of hours in activities they adore, purely for the fun of it, tend to be happy and well-adjusted."[57] The "right content" is unique to each child, and a home-based educational setting provides an ideal opportunity for determining what that content is and retaining it so it's accessible when needed.

The "Right" Time

While it's true that there are optimal windows of opportunity for proper brain maturation when it comes to physical development (e.g., vision or language), the readiness of an individual child for learning academic content during their K–12 career is not as clear-cut. In the book *The Case Against Homework*, Steve Nelson, head of the progressive Calhoun School in New York City, is quoted as saying, "The evidence shows very clearly that kids learn different skills at different times, just like they learn to walk and talk at different

54. Marilee Sprenger, *Learning & Memory: The Brain in Action*. (Alexandria, VA: Association for Supervision and Curriculum Development, 1999), 49.

55. Adam Fletcher, "Giving Students Ownership of Learning," *Educational Leadership* 66 no. 3. (November 2008), http://www.ascd.org/publications/educational-leadership/nov08/vol66/num03/The-Architecture-of-Ownership.aspx.

56. Vicki Abeles and Grace Rubenstein, *Beyond Measure: Rescuing an Overscheduled, Overtested, Underestimated Generation* (New York, NY: Simon & Schuster, Inc., 2016), 147.

57. Abeles and Rubenstein, *Beyond Measure*, 53.

times." The authors add, "When kids of any age are forced to perform tasks before they're developmentally ready, it can open up a Pandora's box of serious problems."[58]

Reading is a common example. Depending on the parent or teacher you ask, you might find that kids naturally begin reading anywhere from around age three to age ten. The conventional school system, however, essentially sets a "correct" time frame for learning this skill even though it's widely recognized that the "normal" range is quite broad. So early readers wait while others catch up, and kids who are not reading by first grade will quickly fall further and further behind, not just in reading but in other subjects as well. In actuality, there is no one "right" age to teach reading—only a "right" age for each *individual*. Looking for signs of readiness or disability and customizing reading training accordingly is the most effective way to reach each child where they are. Even in subjects such as math, where skills typically progress in a very linear fashion, there is plenty of room for natural curiosity and necessity to guide the best timing for each child.

Ogata, quoted earlier, gave us the language to describe the truly "right" time for a student to learn something. It's when they are curious and ready to engage and their interest level is high. Most educators recognize this, but many are limited in their ability to follow the rabbit trails of a classroom full of diverse students' curiosities. The low student-to-educator ratio and freedom available to homeschoolers allows home education to be a nimble, flexible method that can leverage the teachable moments to maximize effectiveness.

The "Right" Method

In their book *Beyond Measure*, authors Vicki Abeles and Grace Rubenstein provide numerous examples of school reforms and methods that seem to be achieving greater effectiveness in traditional and alternative classrooms.[59] In case after case, the recommendations

---

58. Bennett and Kalish, *The Case Against Homework*, 103.
59. Vicki Abeles and Grace Rubenstein, *Beyond Measure: Rescuing an Overscheduled, Overtested, Underestimated Generation* (New York, NY: Simon & Schuster, Inc., 2016).

they give for improving student success and engagement are aligned with the benefits of homeschooling. Among the things mentioned are flexible scheduling, control over sleep times, flex-periods to meet students' unique needs, elimination of homework, longer block class periods to encourage deeper study, integration of subjects, no bells, homework-free holiday breaks, optional self-guided projects, engaging with the outside world, not grading quizzes and tests, internships, customized curricula, multi-age classrooms, "looping" (i.e., having the same teacher for more than one year), mindfulness and mental health breaks, student-led learning communities around common interests, students planning activities, one-on-one interactions, and small class sizes.

Sir Ken Robinson, writer, speaker, and cultural leader, comes to similar conclusions in his educational research. Throughout his book *Creative Schools*,[60] he summarizes ways that classrooms and schools are changing to improve their methods. Much of what he describes as improvements are already true of the homeschool setting. According to Robinson, adaptability and creativity are keys to the success of creative schools. These schools recognize and accommodate the diverse, multifaceted intelligence of their student body and individualize the school experience based on the students' particular interests, strengths, and learning rates. Flexible schedules allow children the space and time to discover their passions, as does an emphasis on unstructured play. Ultimately, the creative, successful classrooms are ones that are moving away from passive, lecture-based models towards more flexible frameworks that empower the student and encourage them in their self-directed learning.

Another area of considerable debate is the traditional school emphasis on high-stakes testing—tests whose results are integral in making important determinations about students' grade promotions or teachers' bonuses, for example. Much to the dismay of many parents and students (as suggested by the growing opt-out movement),

---

60. Ken Robinson, *Creative Schools: The Grassroots Revolution That's Transforming Education* (New York, NY: Penguin Random House, 2015).

testing is still the most common method of K–12 assessment in the United States and many other countries. Being as intertwined with curriculum standards, educators' evaluations, school funding, and data collection as testing now is, it's clear that this method of assessment will continue to weigh down traditional schools in the foreseeable future.

Homeschools are better able to use testing as it was originally intended to be used, that is, as supplementary information rather than as the main source of performance evaluation. As Daniel Koretz discloses to us in his book *The Testing Charade*, "Some of the people who were most influential in the development of standardized testing, and whose professional reputations and incomes depended on the tests they sold, warned that we should *never* use test scores precisely the way they are now used" (emphasis in original).[61] Home educators, even those with state testing requirements to meet, can minimize time spent teaching to the test and are free to also use other creative means for assessment of understanding and performance evaluation. Glasser reminds us that "it would be extremely difficult to come up with an exact definition of quality education that would apply to all situations … however, we can almost always recognize quality when we see it … what is similar about all this [high-quality] work is that none of it could be graded or evaluated by machines— quality never can."[62]

Achieving the Vision

The authors quoted above are just a sampling of those whose stories and research demonstrate the effectiveness of alternative schooling features readily available in the homeschool model. Even in books unrelated to education, it's generally easy to find clues as to how homeschooling continues to produce bright, well-adjusted, and successful students.

---

61. Daniel Koretz, *The Testing Charade: Pretending to Make Schools Better.* (Chicago, IL: University of Chicago Press, 2019), 18.
62. Glasser, *The Quality School,* 6.

For example, Stephen R. Covey, in his well-known book *The 7 Habits of Highly Effective People*, defines the three integral parts necessary for establishing powerful, beneficial habits in our lives. These critical components are "knowledge, skill, and desire" and, he explains, "in order to make something a habit in our lives, we have to have all three."[63] Book learning ("knowledge") and practical training ("skills") can be obtained in many settings, but a home-based education allows for all this to be done in closer alignment with the student's internal motivations and aspirations (that is, their "desire[s]"). By naturally weaving together all three of Covey's components, homeschools set the foundation for students to build healthy academic and personal habits, even from a very young age.

With an emphasis on individuality, depth of learning, original ideas, relationships, and unique experiences, homeschooling clearly has the ability to achieve the vision of the ideal learning setting described below:

"What would an ideal school look like? A kind of school that goes deep instead of wide, that capitalizes on children's particular strengths and tends to their weaknesses rather than putting them all through the same paces, and that asks every student to cultivate truly original ideas instead of mere right answers? A school like that would value quality over quantity, encouraging students to persevere through challenging work that actually means something important to them. It would show high-and low-performing students alike that they can accomplish feats of intellect and creativity they never knew they could. It would frame learning as a rich and varied experience, not a transactional equation. Ultimately, a school focused on learning through vigorous, genuine inquiry would grow the kind of inventive thinkers and keen communicators that our children's futures will demand."[64]

---

63. Stephen R. Covey, *The 7 Habits of Highly Effective People: Powerful Lessons in Personal Change* (New York, NY: Simon & Schuster, 1989), 47.

64. Abeles and Rubenstein, *Beyond Measure*, 154.

Fish Don't Climb Trees

Glasser also brings up a very important caveat about the success of unconventional educational methods and alternative schools. He summarizes the potential and observed effectiveness of magnet schools due to the increased flexibility in school structure (as opposed to a traditional, more rigid structure) like this: "[In magnet schools] teachers can teach more of what they enjoy, and students can learn more of what interests them. When this occurs, there is no need for coercion." He cautions, though, that "magnet schools and other structurally innovative schools can fail *if traditional coercive management prevails*" (emphasis added).[65]

For example, a magnet school, with a more individualized, interest-led learning approach, might encourage students to create exceptional portfolios of quality artwork and outstanding writing samples which, by their very nature, cannot be measured on a standardized test. If the administrators of this "innovative" school continue to judge quality and success by the standardized test measures used in their public school district, not only will the exceptional portfolio work "not count" but the test scores may actually be lower at the magnet school since the students spent their time on untestable pursuits rather than being taught the tested material.[66]

This phenomenon is the same in homeschools whose leaders, typically mom and/or dad, are clinging to the public school paradigm to which they are accustomed. Despite all I've just said about the effectiveness of parent-educators and homeschooling advantages, one of the most certain ways to hinder the potential of your own homeschool is to try to squeeze it into the traditional schooling framework without acknowledging that a homeschool education is its own unique undertaking. It's like trying to judge a (homeschooled) fish by its ability to climb a (public school) tree.

When I was a new homeschooling mom, I assumed that the best first step as a "homeschooling teacher" was to read books meant for

---

65. Glasser, *The Quality School*, 9.
66. Glasser, *The Quality School*, 9 (paraphrase).

new teachers to find answers to my most pressing questions which were, "What do I actually *do* on Monday?" and "How do I do it?" At the time, I was still misunderstanding my new role in the same way many in the non-homeschooling population do. I thought I needed to *become* a classroom teacher and I attempted to do so by impersonating memories of my own favorite elementary school teachers. I tried my best to follow the advice in books like *Tips for New Teachers*[67] and others like it. After hours spent creating lesson plans, researching record-keeping methods, coordinating my lessons with various recommended sequences and state standards, and scouring books such as *What Your First Grader Needs to Know*,[68] all I had to show for my effort were stacks of paperwork, sleep deprivation, and the unshakable feeling that this wasn't going to work.

· · ·

If homeschoolers spend their time seeking God's will for their homeschool, studying their own family's needs, and improving their own methods, it becomes readily apparent how the homeschooling process can be incredibly satisfying and effective.

· · ·

It wasn't until I began to let go of my assumptions about the way school "should" be that I started to realize the true potential of what homeschooling *could* be. The conventional tools and methods aren't necessarily bad; they're just often out of context in a home setting. Take grading, for instance. It didn't take long before I realized the complex grading spreadsheets I'd created for several subjects were simply unnecessary for our homeschool. Although there are home-

---

67. Sue O'Connell, *Tips for New Teachers: Helpful Hints for a Successful School Year* (Columbus, OH: Frank Schaffer Publications, 2001).
68. E. D. Hirsch, Jr., *What Your First Grader Needs to Know: Fundamentals of a Good First-Grade Education* (New York, NY: Bantam Books, 2014).

schoolers who use grades, and grading is a tool that has its place, in our home I find it easier and more meaningful to assess comprehension and retention through our daily interactions. If my kids understand the material and can apply it when needed, we move on. If not, we review in different ways until the information clicks.

Just like anyone who's trying to be something they're not, if a homeschooling parent attempts to morph their situation or personality into something it isn't, they'll likely always feel that their efforts are futile. At the very least, they'll be left wondering what they're doing wrong. Instead, if homeschoolers spend their time seeking God's will for *their* homeschool, studying their *own* family's needs, and improving their *own* methods, it becomes readily apparent how the homeschooling process can be incredibly satisfying and effective.

8

Effectiveness of the Results

Even after we recognize that homeschoolers can be educated effectively by their parents and that there is no such thing as a one-size-fits-all education, some people still question whether homeschoolers will be prepared for the "real world" (there's that term again). Potential homeschooling parents worry that a nontraditional path will cause problems for college admission, job applications, acceptance into the military, or other future endeavors. I, too, wondered at first whether I would be doing my kids a disservice by homeschooling them. After all, schools have built-in resources, information, transcripts, guidance counselors, and proper channels for helping kids move towards their post-graduation goals. How could I, as a homeschooling mom, possibly navigate the complex requirements and replicate all that support and documentation in our home? Even if I could, would anyone take my kids' homemade transcripts and academic achievements seriously? Let's tackle the straightforward questions first.

College Admissions

According to the Home School Legal Defense Association (HSLDA), "homeschool graduates across the country have the right to attend the college of their choice. Home education is legal in all 50 states. Any homeschool that follows the state's requirements governing homeschool programs has the authority to produce valid transcripts and diplomas for its graduates."[69]

However, even though the transcripts and diplomas are valid, some people (including many homeschoolers themselves) find the idea of an accurate, unbiased, "parent-generated transcript" to be untenable due to the familial conflict of interest. How can we really know that Jenny's straight A's don't just mean easy coursework or a protective mom who rounds up to make herself and her child look good? And, as far as class rank is concerned, it's easy to graduate first in your class of one. It's no wonder people are skeptical of homeschoolers when traditional metrics are foisted upon an untraditional context.

Keep in mind, though, that this doubt about a homeschooler's transcript implies that the transcripts of public- or private-schooled students are somehow more factual—that only *they* can give an accurate picture of the student's achievement and comprehension. This, as research and my own personal experience shows, is not always true. Within a system that directly or indirectly links educators' careers to student success (test scores, grades, etc.), transcripts often aren't the accurate picture of reality that they purport to be. In fact, as former English teacher John Owens boldly states, "we are lying if we deny that data manipulation is now so widespread in American education that it's systematic."[70]

Now, before I receive nasty emails, I want to be clear that there are certainly many honest teachers, a number of them among my own friends and family. My point is simply that there are accurate transcripts and inaccurate ones in any educational setting: public, private, homeschool, or other. My public junior high school English teacher raised my final course grade of C+ to an A– after my five-minute tearful plea about it being unfair because "I tried really hard and I've never had a C before." How accurate is the GPA that

---

69. Helaina Bock, "Dear Registrar: Did the Cloud Eat My Transcript?," HSLDA website, accessed April 15, 2019, https://hslda.org/content/hs/state/in/20181030-dear-registrar-did-the-cloud-eat-my-transcript.aspx (article no longer available). Access this article by using The Wayback Machine (an initiative of the Internet Archive) at https://web.archive.org.

70. John Owens, *Confessions of a Bad Teacher: The Shocking Truth from the Front Lines of American Public Education* (Naperville, IL: Sourcebooks, 2013), 211.

includes that A–? A college electrical engineering professor of mine readily raised grades for anyone who asked nicely, and several other teachers in high school and college offered so many extra credit opportunities that anyone could legitimately earn an A for the course despite poor performance on tests and quizzes. How meaningful are the transcripts that bear the final grades for these classes?

Ultimately, anytime we try to boil people down to a set of statistics—GPA, grades, test scores, or rankings—to be compared and analyzed, our evaluation will fall short. Students are not numbers. Thankfully, some colleges realize this and give more weight to a wider variety of performance dimensions now than in the past. Essays and short-answer responses, comprehensive e-portfolios, videos of real-life performance, and other alternatives are becoming increasingly accepted by colleges. They provide a more complete picture of a student's aptitudes, accomplishments, and strengths.

The increase in homeschooling and other alternative methods of education, and the technological explosion of the last few decades, has meant more resources and options for college admission than in the past, regardless of educational background. For example, FairTest, an educational organization working to end flawed testing practices, has posted a growing list of test-optional colleges[71] (that is, schools that don't require or don't emphasize SAT and ACT test scores in the application process) which helps public-schooled students who opt out of testing as well as homeschoolers and others.

Traditional methods are available to homeschoolers, too. Home-educated students have achieved success on tests including AP, CLEP, SAT, ACT, and whichever other abbreviations or acronyms might help them jump through the hoops of college admission. Of course, there are still enough administrators and admissions staff who aren't aware of homeschooling laws to keep the lawyers at HSLDA on their toes. But, on the whole, critics and prospective homeschooling parents need not worry about homeschoolers getting into college. It's

---

71. "925+ Top Tier Schools Deemphasizing the ACT/SAT in Admissions Decisions for Fall 2021," FairTest, last modified December 16, 2020, http://www.fairtest.org/sites/default/files/Optional-Schools-in-U.S.News-Top-Tiers.pdf.

the independent learning skills honed, the lifelong passions developed, and the depth of insight gained through their unique educations that will continue to distinguish homeschoolers from other students in the eyes of their admissions counselors.

Career Applications

Years ago, as a sophomore at Penn State University, I attended my first job fair hoping to land an architectural engineering summer internship position. I'd been preparing for weeks, practicing my answers to interview questions, finding the perfect business suit, compiling my references, and studying up on the companies that would be there. I wanted to be ready for whatever questions would be thrown at me to test my aptitude, my academic background, or the veracity of my résumé.

After a few short conversations at other booths, I came across one of the larger firms with which I'd been hoping to interview. After the initial introductions were made, the conversation took on a life of its own. As it turned out, they didn't ask me almost any of the expected questions. Instead, it was my ability to chitchat about deep dish pizza and my willingness to travel to the Chicago area for the position (perfect for me since that was my home) that clinched my first official internship. The company representatives and I clicked almost instantly as we joked about favorite restaurants, hometown hangouts, pet peeves, and other (mostly non-job-related) topics. I'm sure (at least I *hope*) they took a closer look at my résumé after the job fair, but the ten-minute informal banter alone was enough to demonstrate that I'd likely be a good fit within this company's culture.

I tell this story not to suggest that preparation, résumés, and transcripts are unnecessary but to help us keep things in perspective. My own anecdotal experience and that of my friends and family has repeatedly shown that things such as unusual transcript formatting or lack of a "traditional" high-school GPA simply don't make or break the hiring decision. Job offers happen when there's a mutual need and a good fit. Often, networking and research done by the applicant and hiring manager get the process started and the "click" comes more organically after that.

Apparently my experience isn't unique; industry research backs this up as well. Monster, an international online job search website, interviewed 273 managers and 3,286 employees or job seekers in April 2014.[72] "The five most important factors interviewers consider when making a hire" in order from highest to lowest were work experience (36%), first impression (24%), education (12%), qualifications (10%), and references (9%). Did you catch that? The hiring managers interviewed considered first impressions (which included things like ability to hold eye contact, quality of small talk, and strength of handshake) to be *more important* than education!

In the words of Carol Geary Schneider, president emerita of the Association of American Colleges and Universities, "Our employer studies show that employers basically find the transcript useless in evaluating job candidates."[73] And she's referring to the traditional *college* transcript which would likely be the same for both homeschoolers and non-homeschoolers anyway. Once a student is making the transition from college to career, whatever idiosyncrasies might exist on their homeschool (K–12) transcripts are irrelevant. What matters at this point is what skills they've retained and can apply to their work and who they've become as a person.

Ultimately, hiring managers want to know what you can *do*. Can you do the job or not? Are you trainable? Do you play well with others? Does your personality fit with the company culture? Are you respectful, honest, and trustworthy? Will you show up to work on time (or at all)? When we focus on the skills and traits that employers are *actually* looking for in their new recruits, the worries about homeschoolers not being hirable fade quickly. The time and freedom available to homeschoolers to pursue internships, volun-

---

72. "Job Seekers Have Just 385 Seconds to Make a First Impression," Monster, last modified June 13, 2014, http://info.monster.co.uk/first-impressions/article.aspx.

73. Paul Fain. "Competency-Based Transcripts," Inside Higher Ed, August 9, 2013, https://www.insidehighered.com/news/2013/08/09/northern-arizona-universitys-new-competency-based-degrees-and-transcripts.

teer positions, apprenticeships, and other working-world experiences can actually provide them *more* of what employers are really seeking. In many cases, the space and ability to pursue their passions leads to early entrepreneurial opportunities, in which case *they'll* be the ones doing the hiring. Far from being a hindrance to becoming gainfully employed, homeschooling is often an asset that gives students a unique edge that sets them apart from the other applicants in the résumé stack.

Military Jobs

The idea that homeschoolers aren't eligible for military service is simply inaccurate and based on outdated information, as the following quotations will substantiate. In an article on their website, HSLDA clarifies that "homeschoolers can enlist in the military on the same terms as any other high school graduate. Since 1998, HSLDA has been working with the Pentagon and Congress to ensure that patriotic young men and women who wish to serve their nation in the armed forces are free to do so and are not discriminated against because they were homeschooled. After numerous battles, and most recently, congressional amendments to the National Defense Authorization Act in 2012 and 2014, we are finally ready to declare victory." They go on to announce, "The recent legislation passed by Congress and the accompanying Department of Defense policy have eliminated all past problems facing homeschool graduates who wish to enlist."[74]

To hear it straight from the horse's mouth, the Joint Explanatory Statement that accompanies the National Defense Authorization Act for Fiscal Year 2014 states, "graduates of a secondary school, including graduates who receive diplomas from secondary schools that are legally operating or who otherwise complete a program of secondary education in compliance with state law [which includes homeschools], are required to meet the *same* standard of any test,

---

74. "Military," HSLDA website, last modified February 27, 2015, https://hslda.org/content/docs/nche/Issues/M/Military_Issues.asp (article no longer available). Access this article by using The Wayback Machine (an initiative of the Internet Archive) at https://web.archive.org.

assessment, or screening tool used to identify persons for recruitment and enlistment in the armed forces"[75] (emphasis added). In a 2014 Department of Defense memorandum, the assistant secretary of defense summarizes this by writing that homeschoolers will be treated "in the same manner as a graduate of a secondary traditional HS [high school]."[76]

The Real "Real World"

So, it's clear that homeschoolers can get into college or the military and go on to successful careers afterwards. The underlying questions that still remain, though, are less straightforward. Are homeschoolers *really* prepared for adulthood? Are they too different from the rest of society due to their unique upbringing? Will they have learned enough of the "street smarts" needed to live outside the walls of their own home? Has their homeschool education really *effectively* prepared them to fit in and succeed in society? Tying the idea of effectiveness to preparedness for the real world, as these questions do, can cause confusion since both "effective" and "real world" are tricky to define.

The first term, "effectiveness", as noted earlier, can only be assessed if you know, and have some way of measuring, your desired outcome. A true story[77] comes to mind of a woman who spoke at a church conference and shared her family's emotional journey through her daughter's high school years. The sixteen-year-old daughter, who'd been experiencing bullying at her public high school, refused to return to school after a holiday break and ended up attempting suicide rather than going back to face more peer abuse. Thankfully, she was unsuccessful in her attempt to end her life. After that traumatic event, the parents pulled her out of school and homeschooled her for the remainder of the year.

---

75. U.S. Government Publishing Office, *National Defense Authorization Act for Fiscal Year 2014*, December 2013, https://www.gpo.gov/fdsys/pkg/CPRT-113HPRT86280/pdf/CPRT-113HPRT86280.pdf (Title V, Subtitle H, Section 573).

76. National Guard Bureau, *Memorandum for NG J1 RRF: SMOM 14-013, Revision of Enlistment Policy on Education Credentials*, January 27, 2014, https://smtc.dodlive.mil/files/2018/08/SMOM-14-013-ROB-Revision-of-Enlistment-Policy-on-Education-Credentials.pdf.

77. Some details have been changed to protect privacy.

Undeniably, the goals and outcomes suitable for this vulnerable young lady that year were different from the goals of other students. The mom described how a relaxed approach to academics allowed them to focus on their daughter's need for healing in order to restore her mental and emotional health. They acknowledged that her academic achievements looked different than they would've had she pushed through at the public high school. But today the daughter is a thriving, young professional woman, freed from the dark cloud that once enveloped her. Their family absolutely considers her year of homeschooling to have been effective.

Perhaps this example is an extreme circumstance, but in the day-to-day lives of students in all situations and walks of life, we *must* consider the desired outcome and big-picture goals before we can assess the effectiveness of our approach in reaching those goals. What one child needs to thrive and grow into a healthy adult might look very different from the methods that will best help his peers. Temperaments, learning styles, special needs, strengths, and career goals are just some of the many factors that make "effectiveness" mean different things for different people. The main features of homeschooling—individualization, family time, one-on-one instruction, and so on—are continually shown to be correlated with future success across these categorical differences. That is to say, homeschooling is effective for all types of families in all kinds of different situations.

Another reason for homeschoolers' life success can be understood by contemplating the concept of the "real world." People throw this phrase around loosely and we all have a general understanding of what is meant by it. It's the post-school, grown-up, real-life-begins-now world. Some homeschool critics assume that home-educated students are underprepared for life after school, having been (as the stereotype goes) isolated and kept from the usual social opportunities, the latest educational technologies, and people outside their own families.

Homeschool proponents counter that the homeschooling lifestyle is far *more* closely aligned with the "real world" than the Monday-through-Friday experiences of their same-aged, classroom-schooled peers. More time observing and participating in the daily adult experiences of running a household—helping mom in the garden, accompanying dad to the mechanic, comparing prices at the food store, talking with the mail carrier—and the time and freedom to pursue more field trips, apprenticeships, and volunteering jobs allows homeschooled students to experience firsthand the diverse, real-life, daytime activity of our society.

I do agree that homeschooling affords students a tremendous quantity of real-life training both inside and outside of their home; in fact, this is one of the key benefits of the method in my opinion. However, all families would do well to keep in mind that the real world isn't some far-off place we arrive once our eighteen years of preparation have been endured (or, for all the "adultolescents" out there, thirty years of preparation). The real world is every place and

* * *

By any measure that matters, whether academic or otherwise, home education is a very effective educational option that not only prepares kids for life after school but encourages them to strive towards their fullest potential no matter what their age.

* * *

every experience and every day of our lives. It's your kitchen, your neighbor's backyard, your daughter's third-grade classroom, your husband's office building, and the train car that got him there. It's the weddings, the hospital rooms, the vacations, the errands, the daily grind, the precious moments, and every mundane second in between. It's all the times and places you're alone and every minute you're surrounded by others. You entered the real world as soon as you were conceived and it's been shaping and changing you, and vice versa, ever since.

So, then, the real world is simply "the world" and all of us are already in it. The sooner one realizes this—that they're already living their life—the sooner they'll take ownership of their choices and assume the responsibility of moving themselves towards the plans God has for their future. The time, freedom, and unique perspective available to homeschooled kids often allows them to reach this understanding early in their education, which is why it shouldn't be surprising when we hear of their success later in life. Homeschooled kids, on the whole, grow into successful, healthy, well-adjusted adults.

Brian D. Ray, PhD, of the National Home Education Research Institute (NHERI) states, "The home-educated are doing well, typically above average, on measures of social, emotional, and psychological development. Research measures include peer interaction, self-concept, leadership skills, family cohesion, participation in community service, and self-esteem."[78] By any measure that matters, whether academic or otherwise, home education is a very effective educational option that not only prepares kids for life *after* school but encourages them to strive towards their fullest potential no matter what their age.

---

78. Brian D. Ray, "Research Facts on Homeschooling," January 15, 2021, https://www.nheri.org/research-facts-on-homeschooling/. Also see https://www.nheri.org/a-systematic-review-of-the-empirical-research-on-selected-aspects-of-homeschooling-as-a-school-choice/ for additional relevant research.

9

Practicality of the Job Role

Have you ever had this type of conversation with your son or daughter or maybe with your own parents when you were a kid?

Child: Can I play video games?
Parent: Sure you *can* … but you *may* not.

As a child, I thought it seemed cruel of my parents to use the nuances of English grammar against me, but now, as a parent myself, I find the distinction important and I enjoy pointing it out to my own kids from time to time. The word "can" refers to one's ability to do something, whereas the word "may" expresses permission being granted. In the example above, the child "can" play video games; that is, she has the *ability* to push the controller buttons and play the game. But according to the parent, and much to the child's chagrin, she "may" not; that is, she isn't *allowed* to play video games at that moment.

So far in this book, we've explored the two biggest misconceptions about homeschooling, namely opportunity and effectiveness. In effect, we've been answering the question, "*May* I homeschool?" And the answer (in the United States and many other countries) is, "Yes, you *may* homeschool." It's legal, it's effective, and it's full of opportunities for socialization and academic growth. It's a perfectly legitimate method of education so, yes, you are *permitted* to do it.

We'll now be switching gears to address the very common fears and assumptions people have about the practicality of homeschooling. We'll be asking and answering the question, "*Can* I homeschool?" Or, to put it another way, "Do I have the *ability* to homeschool?" Fortunately, once you really begin to grasp the implications of the information in the previous chapters, the seemingly unconquerable hurdles to homeschooling become much more approachable and very much surmountable.

Just Another Job? Yes and No

In our first few years of home educating, I struggled to pin down my job title. I tried to define it in terms of other professions and put it in a box that I and others better understood. I felt lost without a straightforward answer to the universal grown-up question, "What do you do for a living?" I knew I was waking up each morning and working. But I still wasn't sure how to respond when people asked me what my job was. I recall once taking an inordinate amount of time to fill out the "occupation" question on a consumer survey. Was I a homemaker? Yes, but more than that. Teacher? Sort of, but not exactly. Tutor? Getting closer, I think. School administrator? Well, legally in Illinois, yes. Small business owner/entrepreneur? In a way. Fortunately, there was an "other" box, and I left it at that. Unfortunately, you can't reply "other" when people ask you what your job is in casual conversation.

Early on, I had several interactions with acquaintances who seemed confused when I said I'm a homeschooling mom. If you say you're an architect or a web designer or a doctor, people have a general understanding of what that means. At least they know enough about the job to ask a follow-up question or continue the conversation. But some of the early reactions I got made me question whether what I was doing was a "real" job. At the time, I hadn't yet built up confidence in my own role and didn't have the experience to know what it would fully entail, so it was hard to give my job an official title or explain much of my role to others. If I didn't understand it myself, how could I expect anyone else to?

Having done this a little longer now, I can confidently answer "home educator" when people ask what my day job is. Just as a landscape architect doesn't describe his or her role as "kind of like a building architect but for plants, and sort of like a gardener but without as much digging," the homeschooling parent's job doesn't need to be described in terms of other jobs either. "I'm sort of like a teacher and school administrator who works from home and only teaches her own kids, but I teach them more like a tutor ..." No. Home educator is a job in its own right. And if people don't understand what the term means, we can confidently explain our role further.

⋯

As soon as a person becomes a parent, their homeschooling journey begins.

⋯

Though it is a job, however, it's not *just* another job. Homeschooling, in the sense that it means guiding, training, and educating your own kids, is a "job" that transcends the mere nine-to-five meaning of the term. In this more fundamental sense, *all* parents are homeschoolers. They've just chosen to delegate their job duties in different ways. In their book, *Homeschool Your Child for Free*, authors LauraMaery Gold and Joan M. Zielinski describe it this way. "All good parents homeschool their children. Some do it full time. Some do it part time in partnership with professional educators. And some do it while their kids are on break from traditional schools. If you teach your children at all, you homeschool."[79]

Many parents have been lulled into thinking that education is the duty of the government's school system. In actuality, as soon as a person becomes a parent, their homeschooling journey begins.

---

79. LauraMaery Gold and Joan M. Zielinski, *Homeschool Your Child for Free* (New York, NY: Three Rivers Press, 2009), 1.

Parents teach and guide their child as she learns to sit, eat, walk, talk, use the toilet, play fairly, and tie her shoes—and then they send her off to school because they think that's what they're "supposed" to do. They actually *stopped* a portion of their homeschooling and, wittingly or unwittingly, *chose* a different educational method by sending their child to public school. In actuality, those parents—all parents—are still *fully responsible* for their child's education.

This idea hits close to home for me because I was the unwitting parent. I was on track to pick out a daycare, sign up for a preschool, and follow the neighbors to the bus stop without even thinking about it. Had I not heard of homeschooling when I did, I never would've known I was making a choice or that there were any realistic alternatives to consider. If I can let even one other family know to consider their options—that they even *have* options—then all the efforts creating this book will have been worth it.

So, then, education is just one of the many responsibilities of parenting in general. It is the responsibility of *all* parents to find resources for their kids to help them learn and grow, to support them and provide for them the things they need to develop into healthy adults, and to help them discern God's plan for their life. Parents might choose public school to meet some educational needs and supplement at home or vice versa. But, either way, it's the parents' duty, both legally and morally, to see that their kids are educated. For *all* parents, it's really just a question of how much of your kids' education you outsource and which aspects you assign to whom.

Flexibility Is the Key

Just as correcting homeschool myths is critical to understanding homeschooled *students'* opportunities, so must the mistaken notions about the profession of home educator be clarified to demonstrate the feasibility of the *parents'* role. I touched on this earlier and we'll dig deeper here.

Think about the following partial description of a common occurrence. It doesn't sound rational to put a seventeen-year-old in a box on wheels and send them hurtling through space at forty-five miles per hour, sometimes only feet away from innocent bystanders. Yet, every day, parents send their teens on errands in the family mini-van. Obviously, there's a fuller, more accurate picture of the situation that parents understand which allows them to hand over the keys.

···

For all parents, it's really just a question of how much of your kids' education you outsource and which aspects you assign to whom.

···

Similarly, when unsure parents or skeptics say that homeschooling is impractical, what they mean is that the image in their head—their vision of what they *think* homeschooling will be like—is impractical. If their image is of a mom stuck at home with her kids 24/7 or of a career change to "classroom teacher" when their talents lie elsewhere, then it's no wonder they'd think it's not realistic. This is exactly what I thought when I was first considering homeschooling. As I mentioned earlier, my first assumptions were that I could never do it since I didn't fit the stereotypical role which, in my mind, was a homesteader with a large family. I also remember thinking, "I work in architecture; I'm not a teacher." I felt I would be throwing away the entirety of my career and talents and stepping into the profession of teaching which, as I admitted earlier, was not my forte.

When we try to sum up an unfamiliar situation or career in a few quick, one-sided thoughts, we miss the full picture and the conclusions we draw will not be accurate. Consider the following three illustrations. Who would willingly want a career that demands crazy hours, high-pressure life-and-death situations, and lawsuits from your unsatisfied customers? What about a job that requires last-minute schedule changes and often causes you to miss out on important family events? How about a profession where you have to work on days other people have off and work-life balance is a constant struggle?

Given just these stereotypical and partial glimpses, none of those three options sounds all that appealing. Yet each year thousands of individuals pursue careers as doctors, pilots, and pastors, respectively. If you look closely at the descriptions above, you can see they're far from complete; they're focused on the negative aspects and they're not even entirely accurate. The idea that all doctors work crazy hours, for example, simply isn't always true. If someone is interested in becoming a doctor, they look past the surface level to really understand the big picture and make an educated decision about their future. It's the same (or should be the same) with prospective home educators. There are pros and cons to any career or calling, but it's important to get your information straight before trying to draw any conclusions.

Home educators define their own job descriptions.

One of the key characteristics of the role of home educator that sets it apart from many other professions is *flexibility*. In many ways, home educators define their own job descriptions. You set your own hours and methods. So, in essence, you can rewrite any of the stereotypes that may be floating around in your head inhibiting your forward progress. As a homeschooling parent, you have *tremendous freedom* to create a situation that takes advantage of your strengths and minimizes the impact of your weaknesses. Here are a few examples[80] of what I mean:

- Amy was an accountant before having kids. She loves spreadsheets, planning, and math and still has some connections to her old accounting clients. Now, as a homeschooling mom, she

---

80. These are compilations of real people. Names and/or small details have been changed to protect privacy.

uses her organizational skills to schedule and keep detailed records of her kids' coursework and extracurricular classes. Given her background, she also enjoys creating tailored math and consumer finance lessons for each of her kids. She's never felt strong in language arts, so she outsources those classes to a local co-op where the kids are taught grammar, writing, and literature by a co-op mom who's an author and a co-op dad who is currently a college literature professor. Amy uses quality, open-and-go curricula for the other subjects. She brings in a little extra cash with some accounting side work, which more than covers the cost of the curricula and co-op classes.

- Joanne never went to college; she married right out of high school and had kids right away. She was concerned her lack of formal education would be problematic if she homeschooled but instead has found the opposite to be true. Her kids are excited to learn and curious about everything since Joanne is often learning alongside them and modeling how to find answers to questions. She's found inexpensive curricula and materials at her library and homeschool book swaps, which have provided more than enough learning resources for her kids to follow all their various interests and develop their own lifelong love of learning. Her parents live nearby and stop over twice a week to do art, sewing, and woodworking projects with their grandkids. Joanne knows that record keeping is important but hates keeping track of the details, so she uses homeschool planning software that makes it easy for her to compile and format the documentation required by her state's homeschooling laws.

- Matt, a former high school history teacher, and his wife Sarah, who works as a nurse, decided to pull their kids out of public school and begin homeschooling. They now share the responsibility of homeschooling their kids, and each continues to work part time in their respective professions as well. Matt focuses on teaching history using a combination of purchased curricula and his own lesson plans. His enthusiasm for his favorite subject is contagious, and now all four kids love history and watch historical documentaries with their dad in their spare time. Sarah and her kids participate in a local science co-op that meets twice a week to do experiments and labs as a group. They study more about the science concepts at home together, and they use an online private school for other subjects with both live and on-demand classes.

I could go on and on with examples, but the point is this: the role of homeschooling parent can be pretty much whatever you need it to be. If you hate planning, there are fully planned, open-and-go curricula that require almost zero parent preparation. If you love writing lessons yourself, go for it! If you, as the old song goes, "don't know much about history,"[81] then use a curriculum that will hold your hand as you go through it with your kids and learn more the second time around. Whether you're excited to teach calculus or want to avoid it like the plague, you *can* homeschool! In general, you can make it work if you focus on your gifts and areas of strength and outsource the subjects or duties that aren't in your wheelhouse.

———————————————————— · · ·

The role of homeschooling parent can be pretty much whatever you need it to be.

———————————————————— · · ·

The Three R's

Although I can picture my younger self balking at what I'm about to say, I assure you that it's true. There are really very few necessary employment prerequisites to becoming a successful home educator. When it comes to homeschooling parents, we've already seen that teaching certificates and other pieces of paper are often completely

---

81. Sam Cooke, "What a wonderful world," *The Wonderful World of Sam Cooke* (Los Angeles, CA: Radio Recorders, 1960).

irrelevant. Also, the role is so adaptable that pinpointing any specific skills or aptitudes that would be required for successful homeschooling in *all* cases is a fool's errand. But, based on what I've seen time and time again in my own homeschooling groups and the larger online homeschool community, there are three traits that all successful homeschooling families seem to share. I think these three characteristics are about the closest we can get to a mandatory prerequisite list for parents considering homeschooling.

. . .

Focus on your gifts and areas of strength and outsource the subjects or duties that aren't in your wheelhouse.

. . .

First, successful home educators are *resourceful* in the broadest sense of the term. Some are resourceful because their lives are literally full of physical resources: money, educational supplies, technology, private tutors, and so on. Others are able to find the resources they need. Knowing or learning how to track down classes, co-ops, and support groups, they are able to obtain whatever help they require. Some homeschooling families are resourceful because they use their own gifts and talents directly to build into their children's education. This would include the history buff teaching history, the former elementary teacher writing lesson plans, the engineer teaching the co-op STEM class, and the homemaker coaching kids in cooking or home economics. Most of the homeschoolers I've met are also adept at creating whatever can't be found elsewhere. They think intentionally about their goals and use the library, the internet, their supply closet, their community network—in short, they use any resources at their disposal—to meet their objectives.

The second necessary trait, *responsibility*, is a word I better understood once I watched a *Mister Rogers' Neighborhood* episode on caring for pets. In it, he asks his young audience, "Do you know what responsibility means? It's a big word. But the first part of it, response, is like "answer." You know, when someone says hello to you, you answer that person and you say hello back to them. But when you're taking care of a dog, you need to answer, or respond when the dog is hungry … it's your responsibility to answer to the dog's needs."[82] Being responsible means having the *ability to respond*. All parents are accountable for their children's education and upbringing; they need to find ways to respond to the needs of their kids. Home educators, generally speaking, have chosen to keep some greater degree of their children's day-to-day educational needs under their own control. As such, homeschooling parents need to be able and willing to answer to whatever scope of work they've undertaken.

Finally, behind every choice to homeschool there needs to be a *reason*. We'll talk later about motivation and how varied it is among homeschoolers. But I've yet to meet any homeschooler who home-schools "just because." Intentionality, purpose, and goals are all important aspects of life in general, and it's no different with the choice to educate your kids at home. Knowing the specific reasons behind your choice, knowing *why* you're doing this, will help direct your homeschooling journey and keep you focused.

To the nervous parent considering homeschooling, wondering whether you meet these prerequisites, fear not! The fact that you've found this book and taken the initiative to learn more about something important to you by reading about it demonstrates both *resourcefulness* and *responsibility*. And most people serious enough about homeschooling to research it are doing so because they already have at least one good *reason* (often several).

Also, keep this "career change" decision in perspective. For *most* jobs, the prerequisites aren't as specific and selective as we might assume. At a homeschool seminar I attended, Matt Fowler, president of Wabash Valley College, related that one study in *The Chronicle of Higher Education* found that 78% of employers consider *any* major,

---

82. *Mister Rogers' Neighborhood*, episode 1497, "Pets," 1982, accessed January 19, 2021, https://www.imdb.com/title/tt0810247/quotes/?tab=qt&ref_=tt_trv_qu.

not specific majors, when hiring![83] This is why we often see individuals with a degree in one field building a successful career in an entirely unrelated industry. A relative of mine, for example, obtained an acoustical physics degree and, upon finding no related work after graduation, got a job at a local fast-food place to pay the bills. Years later, he's now rubbing shoulders with the CEO of this well-known restaurant chain as he continues to succeed in that company with no degree in restaurant management, hospitality, or any food industry-related field.

The same is true of homeschooling parents. If you were being interviewed for the position of home educator for your kids, the interviewer would want to know whether you're motivated, responsible, and hardworking. They'd know that most capable, dependable individuals can be brought up to speed on necessary specifics through on-the-job training. If I can speak for the imaginary hiring manager, I'm telling you that if you're willing to jump in and responsibly give it your all, leverage any skills and resources you have, and commit to your work with intentional purpose, then you're hired!

---

83. The Chronicle of Higher Education statistics were presented in person at the 2018 ICHE Conference (Matt Fowler, June 1, 2018, "Portfolios = Peace of Mind" seminar).

10

Practicality of the Day-to-Day

Even after learning more about the role of home educator and realizing that they would be capable in that role in a general sense, many potential homeschooling parents still have unanswered questions about the feasibility of it all. The concerns I've heard, such as "that just sounds way too hard" or "how would I find curriculum?" or "we can't afford it," cause the parents to stop pursuing it because they feel that homeschooling is just an impractical choice. This saddens me. Not because I think everyone should homeschool, but because I think more families could find success and tremendous fulfillment if they didn't give up on the idea.

Just like with any other job or calling in life, there are real pros and cons that need to be considered. But because modern-day homeschooling is still a relatively small movement, most people only have partial understandings, and sometimes no awareness at all, of what the day-to-day really looks like. They make assumptions, catch glimpses, and then make snap judgments.

To be fair, these judgments are often just a tool people use to categorize information and make sense of their world. How else can we be expected to sift through the enormous amount of information we're bombarded with each day? When it comes to deciding which of the 12,000+[84] careers

---

84. Career Planner has a "list of over 12,000+ job titles and job descriptions" on their website: https://www.careerplanner.com/JobDescSearchTool.cfm.

out there you want to pursue, you *must* categorize and eliminate some options; there's simply not time to do in-depth research on every single one. If someone asked me whether I've ever considered working on an oil rig, my mind, without really knowing much about that profession, immediately jumps to all kinds of reasons why that would be a bad fit for me.

When it comes to most professions, knowing yourself (your talents, passions, calling, and abilities), taking career assessments, and drawing from past experiences is usually enough to ensure that your quick evaluation of career possibilities will be fairly accurate. You can efficiently narrow down the huge selection and focus your time researching your most likely options.

However, since the role of home educator is not just a day job but, instead, is intrinsically linked to a key responsibility of parenting, I don't think we can dismiss it as freely as we might when examining other potential career opportunities. All parents have the right and responsibility to investigate all of the available educational options for their kids so that the most suitable choice can be made for each child. Because this educational option happens *also* to be a part-time or full-time job for at least one parent *and* a new lifestyle for the entire family, it, along with other educational alternatives, should be evaluated thoroughly.

It's Just Too Hard

For those of you who still have questions about the feasibility of homeschooling but aren't giving up on the idea yet, good job! This is exactly the kind of perseverance and resolve that will help you in your homeschool! There are definitely real questions that need to be answered or at least considered before you jump in. Throughout the next few sections, we'll take a quick look at some of the common specific doubts parents have about the viability of homeschooling.

If I had a nickel for every time I've heard "I could never homeschool" from a non-homeschooler, well, I'd have at least a dollar. Not quite as popular as questions about socialization, but definitely ranking high, is the idea that homeschooling is just way too hard. Impossibly hard. Too hard because I don't know trigonometry. Too hard because I'm not a teacher. Too hard because I'm tired just thinking about how to get started.

Yes, it is hard. But so are a lot of things. Marriage is hard. Parenting is hard. Getting up for a desk job every morning to put food on the table is hard. Getting kids dressed, fed, and onto the bus every school day by 7:30 a.m. for thirteen years is hard. Dealing with bosses and clients who expect the unreasonable is hard. Working at home, working part time, and working full time are all hard. Work is hard. Life is hard.

Homeschooling is just another, different kind of hard thing. It's one that you'll get used to just like you would if you started a new career or new relationship or went through any other life transition. I used to deal with the difficulties of the corporate world: stressful meetings, unforgiving deadlines, angry clients, and high-pressure decisions. Now my stressful meetings are math lessons with my son who'd rather be playing Minecraft. The many small deadlines have been replaced with one gigantic, looming deadline called "graduation." My angry clients throw mac 'n cheese instead of slamming tables with their fists. As for the high-pressure decisions, I still have those, too. And none of us, in any profession, has the ability to know what might've been had we decided differently.

So, is one of those scenarios worse than the other in terms of difficulty? I honestly don't know. There are days when I'd give anything for a peaceful, quiet, hour-long commute to somewhere … anywhere! There are other days when I'm so grateful for the chance to snuggle with my kids on the sofa while we read great books and sip hot cocoa, and I can't imagine loving my life any more than I do at that moment. When I worked full time, I would've given anything for a chance to read a book on the couch in the middle of a weekday afternoon and my hour-long commute was a daily headache.

"If we take a step despite feeling uncomfortable, afraid, or inadequate, our comfort zones expand. We grow in strength and skill. What we consider normal for us changes, sometimes radically," state

Alex and Brett Harris in their book *Do Hard Things*.[85] I'd encourage parents to consider homeschooling in this light. Don't make your decision for or against homeschooling by only looking at a list of the hard things the job will entail. If people made all their decisions that way, none of us would accomplish much. We certainly wouldn't decide to have kids! Interrupted sleep, poopy diapers, the crushing weight of the responsibility for another's well-being, zero privacy, no paid sick days, no unpaid sick days, in fact, no breaks at all. … Who would ever choose to be a parent based on this list?

If there are reasons why homeschooling would likely be a good fit for your kids and your family, if it's something God has called you to, then move forward with the confidence that you will be equipped as needed. The great freedom of homeschooling gives parents the ability to compensate for, and to strengthen, their real or perceived weaknesses. It allows them to minimize or outsource the aspects of the job they'd rather not deal with and focus their efforts on the parts they enjoy and are good at.

So to answer the original question, is it hard? Yes. Is it *too* hard? No.

It's Just Too Overwhelming

The previous section was directed at non-homeschoolers who think they could never homeschool because it's too hard. I'd like to speak now to those of you who *are* homeschooling but feeling utterly overwhelmed. Maybe you've pulled your teen out of public school and are one week in and feeling as though you're drowning. Or maybe you've thought about it for a long time, but now that you've "officially" started the walls feel like they're closing in on you and you're not sure whether you can do it.

First of all, you're not alone. The decision to homeschool is significant and impacts most, if not all, areas of every homeschooling family's life. I don't know of any homeschoolers who didn't have some kind of bumpy transition period. Even the most extreme

---

85. Alex Harris and Brett Harris, *Do Hard Things: A Teenage Rebellion Against Low Expectations* (Colorado Springs, CO: Multnomah Books, 2013), 67.

unschooling family, whose natural, child-led approach to starting "school" is indistinguishable from the flow of their life, will *still* have seasons of adjustment as kids reach new ages and stages and their family's needs change.

Again, just like a lot of worthwhile things in life, homeschooling can become overwhelming if we let it. There can also be seasons of life when everything seems to fall apart at the same time through no fault of our own. I, for one, found myself extremely overwhelmed when we started homeschooling. I had no idea how to write lesson plans, choose one curricula over another, find a co-op, or be with another human 24/7 and stay sane. Or did I?

I assumed I couldn't do any of those things because I hadn't done those specific things before, but I was too anxious to remember that I had a lot of personal experience I could apply to this new situation. For example, I'd never compared curricula or co-ops before, true. But I *did* have a lot of experience making educated decisions. I'd compared hundreds of products before purchasing, I'd evaluated insurance companies before signing up, I'd researched homes and neighborhoods before buying a house, and I'd analyzed a half-dozen colleges before selecting one. As it turns out, it's really no different selecting curricula and homeschool groups.

The misconceptions we've discussed also played a part in my anxiety. I was worried I wouldn't be able to handle being with my kids 24/7. But, as I began to see how much flexibility homeschoolers have to find a balance that works best for their family, my overwhelm decreased. When I tried writing my own lesson plans for several subjects and re-creating public school at home, homeschooling was so overwhelming that I wanted to quit. But as I let go of my ideas about what school "should" be like, again my anxiety decreased and homeschooling became more enjoyable.

I don't know your specific situation, but the following general recommendations might help make things more manageable. First, don't walk the homeschooling path alone! Doing *any* job without co-workers, mentors, or friends is a recipe for disaster. Find a support group or co-op with people who can walk with you and share the journey. If you don't know of any, ask around at churches, libraries, schools, and park districts and search online until you find other local homeschoolers and start making connections. Don't worry if you don't find a new best friend in the first week or even year. Relationships take time, and you've got to start somewhere.

Next, take a look at your specific sources of overwhelming feelings. Are you unable to find the resources you think you need? Do you *really* need them? I found that a lot of my own initial worries were totally unnecessary. I was trying to find the right high school grammar curriculum when my oldest was in kindergarten! I put way too much pressure on myself to have *all* the answers for *all* the subjects for *all* the years for *all* my kids. Please, if this sounds like you, take a deep breath (or ten) and focus on one next step you can take today. Just one. You can set aside times for researching ninth-grade grammar in the future. For now, just make some cocoa, read a few picture books with your kids, and call it a day (a *less-stressed* day).

Or, do your overwhelming feelings stem from you trying to work outside your areas of giftedness? Like the authors of *Do Hard Things* just reminded us, it can be a good thing to stretch yourself and step outside your comfort zone. But if you're paralyzed with fear and anxiety, it may be a sign that you need to find another way to do something. Maybe take a *smaller* step out of your comfort zone. Maybe focus on actions that better align with your talents and experience. As I said, writing my own lesson plans wasn't working for me at all. Instead of forcing something that clearly wasn't working, or giving up on homeschooling altogether, I switched to using resources that included pre-prepared lessons. It was a relatively easy change, and it completely reshaped my homeschool experience. Instead of throwing in the towel on homeschooling, analyze the root of your apprehension. In most cases, you'll find a solution or next step that will allow you to carry on and flourish.

If you moved to a new country, I'm sure you wouldn't expect to have the language, customs, maps, and routines all figured out in the first week. If you still had an accent or only one or two new friends after the first year, that would be completely reasonable. Feeling comfortable after such a significant transition simply doesn't happen overnight. The same is true of homeschooling. Give yourself the same grace, compassion, and time to get accustomed to the changes as you'd give a new neighbor from abroad.

Who Has the Time?

Another common charge against homeschooling is that it's just too time-consuming, to the point of impossibility. How does anyone have the time to plan out and implement all the school subjects with multiple kids or even one child? Here, again, we see misconceptions underneath this question. It's absolutely true that no one could teach their five-year-old kindergarten subjects for a few hours, then teach their elementary twins a full six-hour day of fifth grade, and then teach their junior high student for another seven hours. Fortunately, real homeschooling doesn't look anything like that.

Home education itself, like tutoring, is an extremely efficient model for education. The efficiency of a student being individually guided—as they learn at their own level, review only when necessary, and move forward as soon as they're able—cannot be overstated. Even just cutting out the daily classroom time-wasters such as lining up for gym class or passing out papers to thirty students adds up. By using one-room schoolhouse techniques and combining ages for subjects like history and science, homeschoolers not only save time but also provide the enriching benefits associated with mixed-age learning.

The sooner a new homeschooler can let go of the urge to recreate a traditional classroom schooling experience, the sooner a whole world of time-saving opportunities becomes available to them. Learning through life experiences is easily one of the most popular time-saving strategies utilized by many homeschooling families. Said another way, separating learning from home life is one of the biggest time-wasters of the traditional schooling method. Here's what I mean.

In traditional schools, artificial learning environments are created to *replicate* existing home environments and train students for future, grown-up-life situations. My public-school, seventh-grade home economics classroom, complete with sinks, ovens, and sewing machines, was created to train students in basic cooking and sewing skills. My high school economics class gave us pseudo checkbooks to practice money management and budgeting. In health class, our favorite project was carrying around an egg in a basket for a week to better understand what it's like to be a parent. At the end of each day, when kids come home from school and parents come home from work, there are still meals to be made, bills to be paid, and sibling relationships to nurture.

———————————————————— · · ·

Separating learning from home life is one of the biggest time-wasters of the traditional schooling method.

———————————————————— · · ·

In our homeschool, we learn how to cook by cooking meals. My kids learn about money by counting and managing their own real money to see whether they have enough to buy the latest overpriced electronic gadget yet. And they've witnessed and participated directly in the day-to-day care of their younger siblings (a much more realistic lesson in parenting than babysitting a raw egg). We get real, necessary chores done while learning the life skills and academic lessons to do them well. On top of that, we're building strong family bonds and honing character all at the same time. That's killing a half-dozen birds with one stone!

Keep in mind, too, once you recognize that "classroom teacher" and "homeschool parent" are different roles, you'll begin to see all the work you *don't* have to do that is often part of a traditional schoolteacher's job. The time I do *not* have to spend on these duties—decorating bulletin boards, managing weekly forms, organizing paperwork for dozens of students, or grading twenty-five seven-paragraph essays—I can spend on other necessary tasks or time with my family. One public school teacher friend of mine told me it takes her an entire week of evenings plus a full weekend just to fill out report cards and prepare documentation for parent-teacher conferences. Although I have been known to talk to myself on occasion, I haven't yet gone so far as to host my own homeschooling parent-teacher conferences, so that's yet another task *not* on my to-do list.

When it comes to the planning homeschooling parents *do* need to do, remember that you don't have to reinvent the wheel unless you want to. There are complete boxed curricula, online programs, and co-op groups (both online and in person) that provide everything you'd need to homeschool with almost no detailed planning required. If you find one that's a good fit but you want to tweak the content, go for it. I tend to let the curricula I've selected do the legwork and then I supplement and customize it for my own kids. If you'd rather pull together or create lesson materials by individual subject, that works, too. No matter what amount of time you have available to dedicate to the administrative side of homeschooling, through trial and error you'll find a good balance.

There are a number of other helpful time-saving strategies homeschooling parents pick up along the way to address specific time-draining issues. Older kids can read to younger kids. Audiobooks can be great ways to read and learn on car rides or when reading aloud isn't possible. Field trip and activity planning can be shared among co-op parents. Home management software and homeschool planners help minimize wasted time by helping parents stay organized. Homeschool schedules can be modified to take advantage of peak learning times for students so that less time is wasted with dawdling and complaining. Planning ahead during summer months frees up weekends and evenings during the school year. And by training their older kids to work independently, home educators teach important lessons in responsibility while also saving time.

Before I had my first child, I spent hours upon hours, months in advance of his birth, researching and reading about types and brands of diapers. By the time my third baby was born, I knew from experience that I could just send my husband to pick up whatever diapers were on sale and we'd be fine. Just like caring for a newborn, you'll get better at homeschooling with practice and experience. You'll find out about more time-saving ideas to implement. You'll also get faster at your work and become more familiar with various curricula and opportunities available to you, so narrowing down and implementing options won't be as time-consuming.

Are there times I have to skip watching an episode of my favorite TV show with my husband in order to clean up our schoolroom and find the supplies for tomorrow's science experiment? Sure. Just like my non-homeschooling friends have to sacrifice some of their evening time to help with homework or make school lunches. We all have twenty-four hours in a day at our disposal. Does homeschooling take up some of that time? Yes. Most worthwhile things do.

Money Matters—Part 1

Money is a real issue. That's not to say the other concerns we've discussed aren't important, too. But finances, more than the other issues, are very concrete. There's a bottom line that must be met, and numbers don't lie. You might be able to change your mindset when it comes to deciding whether homeschooling is too hard or overwhelming for you to tackle. But it's not as easy to create money where there isn't any.

There are two different aspects to the "we can't afford to homeschool" concern. The first is something that can be addressed fairly easily. The second is more difficult but not impossible to deal with. Let's start with the lower-hanging fruit.

In 2017, public schools spent $12,201[86] per student per year in the United States, according to the U.S. Census Bureau. It's easy to see a number like that and assume that that's the per-student cost because that's what it actually costs to educate a student. Well, that may be what *public schooling* has to cost (a separate debate entirely), but it certainly isn't what *education* needs to cost.

---

86. U.S. Census Bureau, *U.S. School Spending per Pupil Increased for Fifth Consecutive Year,* U.S. Census Bureau Reports, May 21, 2019, https://www.census.gov/newsroom/press-releases/2019/school-spending.html.

The distinction between education and schooling has been made in different ways by different people. Albert Einstein wryly said it like this: "Education is what remains after one has forgotten what one has learned in school."[87] Mark Twain similarly remarked, "I never let schooling interfere with my education."[88] Schooling, in the traditional sense that we understand it in our culture today, is one method of educating. Education is a broader concept that involves the true learning and knowledge one obtains throughout life in ways that may or may not include a school classroom.

Though schooling may have a significant price tag, education does not. Education can be free or, at least, as inexpensive as you want to make it. There have been years my own family has spent a few hundred dollars *total* to educate my three kids. Other years it's been more, due mainly to extracurricular activities and private lessons (some of which they'd be taking even if we didn't homeschool). I know homeschoolers who've spent next to nothing by using their library card, a guidebook like *Homeschooling on a Shoestring*,[89] and the abundance of free resources available online. Do a quick internet search on homeschooling for free and you'll see what I mean.

Just like any other area of life, there are trade-offs between convenience and cost. But even high-quality, prepackaged, comprehensive boxed curricula are available for hundreds of dollars per student per year, not tens of thousands. To further reduce the financial impact of purchasing educational materials, many homeschooling families use resources for multiple siblings and sell their non-consumable curricula when finished. The cost of your kids' at-home education can easily be adapted to fit your budget, no matter how big or small.

87. "Albert Einstein Quotes," Brainy Quotes, accessed January 19, 2021, https://www.brainyquote.com/quotes/albert_einstein_108304.

88. "Mark Twain Quotes," Brainy Quotes, accessed January 19, 2021, https://www.brainyquote.com/quotes/mark_twain_145906.

89. Melissa L. Morgan and Judith Waite Allee, *Homeschooling on a Shoestring* (Colorado Springs, CO: Waterbrook Press, 1999).

Money Matters—Part 2

Now for the harder money question. How can we afford to home-school if it means losing an income in our two-income household? As is true for the rest of our homeschooling discussion, there isn't a one-size-fits-all answer to this. For some, it's really a nonissue since the second income is already nonexistent or not critical to making ends meet. Other parents, however, will need to think about this topic in detail to ensure that they're making a wise choice for their family.

When we decided I would stay home with my oldest son, this is one of the questions that kept me up at night. In our situation, it helped that the transition was gradual. At first, when we thought I might be going back to work, it was a little easier to swallow the loss of half our annual household income. We figured we could make it work for six months or a year and then get back to business as usual. But after balancing the budget with our new, lower income, we found that "making it work" actually worked. That is, our new, less extravagant lifestyle not only was fine but quickly felt like "normal" to us.

We were just as content with one or two meals dining out a month as we had been with five or six. We had just as much fun renting Redbox movies and making popcorn as we did watching first-run movies in the theater. We practiced cultivating contentment and, honestly, we found that scaling back our expenses was (and still is) a satisfying and life-giving process.

Dave Ramsey, and probably every other financial expert out there, recommends living within your means as a key to ensuring financial stability. In a nutshell, this mean spending less than you make. Early in our marriage, we'd taken Ramsey's Financial Peace University class,[90] so, when it came time to buy a new home for our growing family, we did what we would've done if we'd had twice as much income. We made the decision to live within our means.

At that time, we were beginning to homeschool my oldest for preschool and we knew, even if we didn't continue homeschooling, I

---

90. For more information about Dave Ramsey and the Financial Peace University program, visit https://www.daveramsey.com.

would stay home with my second child at least through his kindergarten years. This meant that our "means" weren't about to increase anytime soon. And that, in turn, meant that the house we bought (and still live in today) is about half the size and value of the house we could've had if I was working. I've calculated that, even without factoring in raises and bonuses, to date I've given up over $700,000 of income to stay home and homeschool my kids.

And you know what's amazing? I'm at peace with that. God called my family to this path and He's providing ways for us to walk in it. Letting go of our hold on fleeting things—material things—has given our family tremendous freedom and has helped us find joy regardless of our circumstances.

All that to say, my answer to this question might leave you feeling frustrated. The choice to homeschool might mean cutting back on movies and manicures and clipping coupons instead. It might mean finding a part-time job for a season. It might mean bartering childcare for piano lessons. In the more extreme cases, it might even mean selling a car or moving to a new home. If homeschooling is the right path for your family, modifying your financial situation and outlook will probably be required to some degree. But, as you make financial adjustments, remember that doing what it takes to follow the path you know is right for your family will pay back dividends that money never could.

This Isn't What I Pictured

As you consider your educational alternatives, at some point in the decision-making process, you'll find yourself at a fork in the road. Glancing left, you'll see the path that you've already been on continuing per usual. Looking ahead on this path, you see the career plans, yellow busses, and routines with which you've grown comfortable—so comfortable, in fact, that your very identity has become wrapped up in that path. You're the marketing director, the soccer mom, the part-time administrative assistant, or the interior designer. You pretty much know what to expect on this path and you know what will be expected of you.

And it's because of this perception of identity and comfort that turning your gaze to the other path is so unsettling. Looking right, you notice that this second path bends in and out of a grove of thick trees, making it difficult to see where it's going or what you might encounter there. From what you can make out, the trail itself seems undefined, not nearly as well worn as the other one. In some places, it seems to disappear completely, leaving you to forge through tall grass and bushes to make a way through. You wonder how this could possibly be the road for you; you don't even own hiking boots!

The prospect of homeschooling feels like the path on the right to many families, both parents and kids. Parents know they'll be going against a significant societal current, perhaps leaving a career they love, putting bucket-list dreams on hold, and changing routines that they've relied on to manage family life. Kids, especially those who've already attended traditional schools, may worry that they'll lose all their friends, have no social life, and be stuck in their house all day with mom or dad. And kids and parents alike might feel they won't even know who they are anymore, as individuals or as a family, should they take the road less travelled.

Well, if history has taught us anything (the chaos of 2020 comes to mind), it's that we definitely can't predict the future. Our perceived comfort with the path on the left is an illusion. Businesses fail, new opportunities arise, people get laid off, unexpected blessings come our way, birth and death happen, all in timing largely out of our control. In reality, the two paths themselves are *both* shrouded from our view.

As for what can reasonably be expected on the homeschooling path, that's something that can be prepared for to some extent. Practically speaking, many of the home management procedures needed to homeschool successfully are probably already in place and can just be expanded upon. For example, my husband and I have held regular "family meetings" even before we had kids. We set aside some time each month to review our budget, upcoming household projects, and the next month's calendar. As our family grew, the meetings naturally changed to reflect our new season of life. Our budget included new line items like diapers, and our list of household projects started to include things like wiping marker off the walls and scrubbing applesauce off of the minivan ceiling.

Homeschooling is just another natural extension of family life. Once we started educating our kids at home, our meetings continued, but now they included budget amounts for curricula and enrichment classes. Similarly, in other areas of our life (our approach to discipline, our family schedule, our goals, and our ideas for vacations, to name a few), routines were already established or in progress. We simply modified and added to the structure and methods we already used as parents and in life in general.

· · · ─────────────────────────────

You don't lose your personhood or identity if you switch careers or start homeschooling.

· · · ─────────────────────────────

Just like any other significant life choice (like having kids, being a family who travels regularly, or running your own family business), homeschooling can and will have a life-altering effect. But you'll adapt to your new circumstances just like you've adapted to other situations in your life so far. Though it may feel like a change of lifestyle is threatening your very identity, I assure you, you will still be *you* no matter which way you turn at the fork in the road.

Rachel Jankovic tackles the existential "who am I?" question head on in her book *You Who? Why You Matter and How to Deal With It.* If we've allowed ourselves—our very soul and identity—to be defined by personality traits like "introvert" or accomplishments like "successful businessperson," then we'll push back on any person, thing, or opportunity that threatens that self-assessment since we feel it's threatening who we *are.* As Jankovic strongly states, "self-rescue takes precedence over everything, because you have allowed yourself to believe that you are actually being murdered by your situation."[91] That is, you feel your "essential self," *you* in the truest, deepest sense of the word, is being taken from you.

Thankfully, though, this isn't true. You ultimately aren't defined by things you've achieved or who your neighbor believes you are. You don't lose your personhood or identity if you switch careers or start homeschooling. Nor is your true self determined by what the world sees as your essential traits. "Far from being your essential traits," Jankovic tells us, "they are just the chips coming off the block of marble as God shapes you into what He intends you to be."[92]

Final Thoughts on Practicality

It may be that there are significant stressors in your life and it really *isn't* practical or possible to homeschool right now, despite a strong desire to do so. Certainly, if there are dangerous addictions or abusive patterns in your home, or if financial or marital struggles are already a significant burden, it would be best to get help for the current tensions before attempting to add another new life-changing variable into the mix. If you're unsure, please talk to a trusted counselor or pastor who can help you assess your situation and find healing so you can make the wisest decision for your family.[93]

It's also important to keep in mind that just because homeschooling has the potential to help students achieve great success doesn't mean it happens automatically. Just like living in a great school district or hiring the most sought-after math tutor in the city doesn't guarantee success 100% of the time, neither does announcing "we homeschool now" ensure a cakewalk with a storybook ending.

Homeschooling is an educational method and a calling for some, but it's also a job; you will have to work at it. It can feel overwhelming, but it doesn't need to be. It's hard, but not *too* hard. It's time-

---

91. Rachel Jankovic, *You Who? Why You Matter and How to Deal with It* (Moscow, ID: Canon Press, 2019), 146.

92. Jankovic, *You Who?*, 158.

93. If you need help finding a counselor, contact the Focus on the Family counseling specialists by visiting https://www.focusonthefamily.com/get-help/counseling-services-and-referrals/.

consuming, but not impossibly so. And, financially speaking, home-schooling will likely have an impact, but most families can find ways around or through that challenge.

In a general sense, homeschooling, as a lifestyle and educational method, is no less practically possible than any other career, educational method, or way of life. The simple fact that it's less well understood in our culture just makes it seem that way. In actuality, the skill sets you use to adapt and succeed in other areas of life can be the same ones you use to homeschool successfully. You're *not* starting from scratch with an empty backpack, and you're *not* alone on the path. As you stand at the fork in the road, remember that *millions* of other students and families have woven their way through the grove of trees towards the right and have been richly blessed because they did.

So, now that you know you *may* homeschool and are hopefully beginning to realize that you *can* homeschool, the only question left is, *should* you homeschool? As much as I want to help you decide, that's a question I can't answer for you. As you seek God's confirmation, research more about the benefits of homeschooling, and reflect on the needs of your family and kids, I pray that opportunities and answers will come to you, making the choice clear.

11

Motives

Although I'd been reading every book, article, and blog I could find on homeschooling for years, it wasn't until a few months before we started kindergarten with my oldest son that I really felt like it was becoming real for our family. We were becoming one of … them! This was the point when I could sense family and friends, who had patiently endured my naive homeschool-related babbling thus far, leaning in to see whether we'd really go through with it.

The responses from acquaintances changed from, "Oh, interesting idea …" to a much more tense reaction. "I would never consider that. I could never deprive my kids of all the experiences of childhood!" and "Ugh! Just when you could finally get a *break* from them!" (said in front of my kids). Or "That might be fun for the early years I guess. You're not planning on [*scrunchy face of dismay*] continuing when they're older, are you?!"

Even the discussions with my husband reached a new, more strained level. Are we *really* making the right choice? Can we *really* afford to continue on one salary? We were completely inexperienced and very insecure. No longer could we hide from ourselves and others behind a facade of "we're *considering* homeschooling" or "we're looking into our options." After September, we'd have no choice but to answer the question, "Which school does he go to?" with, "We homeschool." The rubber was about to meet the road.

Although we had our reasons for looking into homeschooling in the first place, it was around the time we actually starting homeschooling for kindergarten that the importance of motivation began to become clear to me. Now, years later, I'd say motivation isn't just important—it's a *key factor* in homeschooling success. Parents must know *why* they're doing this, for a number of reasons. Motivation is what drives the homeschool bus in the right direction. It's what keeps you from chasing after every new whim willy-nilly. Your reason—your "why"—is what keeps you from giving up on the hardest days and helps you get started in the first place.

Others might not understand or validate your reasons, and some critics assume the worst. But that just makes it all the more important for homeschooling parents to have prayerfully and thoroughly weighed their options and come to a well-reasoned conclusion about their main purpose for homeschooling.

Bad Motives?

People who have a skewed or inaccurate view of the opportunities and effectiveness available to homeschooled kids understandably view homeschooling parents with suspicion. After all, what kind of parent would knowingly keep their kids from growth opportunities or effective learning experiences? And what type of person would experiment on their own children with what the critic views as an inadequate model of education? Do you see how important a correct understanding of homeschooling opportunities, socialization, and effectiveness is to accurately thinking about home education? Foundational to all subsequent dialogue is an understanding of what home education *really is*.

Once the skeptics shed their inaccurate images and stereotypes about homeschoolers, we can engage in a more productive conversation. Often all that's needed is to look at individual situations instead of trying to make generalizations. (Homeschooling is, by definition, a family-specific lifestyle, so general homeschooling statements are hard to make, even if just for the sake of discussion.) What is considered helicopter parenting by some might be absolutely necessary for the special needs of a certain student. What might be thought of as an insignificant reason by one person is another's main motive for their educational decision.

There are several "bad motive" arguments used to discredit homeschooling, and many of them revolve around inappropriate levels of control or excessive avoidance of the "outside world." Consider the parents chided for taking their student out of school due to a bullying situation. Other parents and school administrators might criticize them as being overprotective. Yet, if the student stays in the dangerous situation and ends up being seriously hurt, these parents would be the first ones blamed—perhaps even prosecuted—for knowing about a problem and not doing something to intervene.

Is a parent in this situation exerting an excessive level of control? The handful of parents I know who have taken kids out of unhealthy school settings aren't being *over*protective—they're just plain protective. As in, they're *protecting* their child—making a responsible choice with the information they have—to keep their child safe. The fact that homeschooling is a legal option is a blessing to the kids for whom school settings really are a dangerous place, whether physically, emotionally, or psychologically. The same can be said for school choice in general. When no one method of education has a monopoly, students and families benefit.

* * *

When no one method of education has a monopoly, students and families benefit.

* * *

I've known other homeschooling parents whose decisions to homeschool were at least partially based on reasons deemed overly avoidant by others. Whether they want to live off-grid or they have kids with serious food allergies, these families have one thing in common: they've thought about their decision. If off-grid, sustainable living is your passion, it's not unreasonable to want to provide an education for your kids that trains them in self-reliant living and minimizes their on-the-grid footprint. Or, if your grade schooler's food allergies put them in potential danger at every meal, it would be irresponsible *not* to put them in a school setting where they can be monitored more closely. Frankly, in a society that purports to embrace diversity and "being true to yourself" as much as ours does, it often surprises me how much pushback some homeschooling families receive when they're attempting to live out their values.

Abuse and Neglect

Of course, any freedom can be misused. We live in a broken world, and we see the effects of human sin all around us. The question for the homeschooling community, then, is no different than the age-old question for our community at large. How do we protect the constitutional rights and innate freedoms of families and individuals while also protecting our citizens' safety and ensuring that justice is served for those who abuse their freedoms? Solving this enduring dilemma is outside the scope of this book, but I will say that any debate around ensuring student health and welfare in homeschool settings must be undertaken by those who truly understand what homeschooling is and is not.

Mass media tends to present one-sided, sensationalized, and oversimplified stories of these complex issues, furthering stereotypes and undue suspicion of homeschoolers. In an effort to present the other side of the story to cultivate a more balanced perspective, I'd encourage you to read *Child Abuse of Public School, Private School, and Homeschool Students: Evidence, Philosophy, and Reason*, written by Brian D. Ray, PhD, and available for free online.[94]

In this short paper, Ray tackles the weighty issue of child abuse in educational settings and presents empirical evidence, research,

---

94. Brian D. Ray, "Child Abuse of Public School, Private School, and Homeschool Students: Evidence, Philosophy, and Reason," January 23, 2018, https://www.nheri.org/child-abuse-of-public-school-private-school-and-homeschool-students-evidence-philosophy-and-reason/.

and an overview of the philosophies and worldviews that affect our understanding of this topic. He discusses the often-proposed solution of additional regulations as the answer to these problems and delves into the true implications and effects of increased government oversight of homeschooling. "People who want the government to control and regulate homeschooling more might have good intentions but they have no empirical evidence to support their claims that more government control will solve any problem." In fact, research has shown that "in families where people were legally homeschooling, there was a significantly *lower* incidence of child fatalities due to child abuse or child neglect" (emphasis added).

Despite clear evidence, ineffective solutions are regularly proposed by policymakers and other influencers (sometimes with noble intentions, sometimes not) that would end up punishing innocent families through unwarranted searches and other "guilty-until-proven-innocent" strategies, all while still not helping the victims of real abuse. As homeschooling continues to increase in popularity, we can be sure more debate will come.

Giving policymakers, educators, and the general public a more accurate picture of homeschooling is a critical step in beginning to solve these complicated issues. Often, when presented with factual information and research, sponsors of heavy-fisted, homeschool-limiting bills retract or table their proposed legislation, having realized the implications of their solution. As faulty logic and misguided assumptions are replaced with actual data and sound reasoning, we can collectively work together to find real, effective solutions to prevent abuse and neglect for *all* children, regardless of their method of education.

The Ultimate Hidden Motive: Brainwashing

Of all the "ulterior motive" arguments I've heard or read, the idea that homeschoolers' main motivation is the brainwashing of their children seems to come up most frequently. Typically this is said in regard to religious beliefs, although not exclusively. This highly volatile topic tends to stir up a lot of emotion because views on this issue are ultimately a result of each individual's underlying worldview.

As the data from the 2012 Parent and Family Involvement in Education Survey of the National Household Education Surveys Program (NHES)[95] shows, "a desire to provide moral instruction" does rank high on the list of reasons parents gave for their decision to home educate, as does "a desire to provide religious instruction." These two reasons were listed as "important" by 77% and 64% of parents, respectively. Interestingly, though, and counter to the notion that most homeschoolers home educate for mainly religious reasons, 91% of parents listed "a concern about the environment of other schools" as an important factor in their decision. The same survey also asked parents what their "most important" factor is. To this question, the top response was the "concern about the environment of other schools" (25%), followed by "other reasons" (21%), "a dissatisfaction with academic instruction at other schools" (19%), and "a desire to provide religious instruction" (17%). So, while religious or moral instruction is important to many homeschooling families, it's one of many factors and isn't even the top reason cited by many homeschoolers themselves.

With that perspective established, how *do* we address the concern that young, impressionable minds might find themselves indoctrinated by their parent-educator's ideas and worldview? Well, we don't need to wonder. We already know the answer. The truth is that all youth are influenced by their teachers, regardless of educational methods used. In their book *Notes on Teaching*, authors Shellee Hendricks and Russell Reich remind teachers to "know that you are teaching values." They state, "Don't ask whether teachers should teach values. They do."[96] In other words, *there is no such thing as neutral.* Everyone has a worldview and holds certain values to be true, even if they don't acknowledge or know that they do. The values and

---

95. U.S. Department of Education, "Homeschooling in the United States: 2012," April 2017, https://nces.ed.gov/nhes/tables.asp (p. 12, table 3).

96. Shellee Hendricks and Russell Reich, *Notes on Teaching: A Short Guide to an Essential Skill* (New York, NY: RCR Creative Press, Inc., 2011), 35.

worldviews of individuals and of systems are propagated intention-ally or unintentionally, by what you teach, how you teach, what you say, what you don't say, what you do, and what you don't do. Any person—teacher, parent, or anyone else—who interacts with a student is directly or indirectly teaching values to that child.

· · ·

Everyone has a worldview and holds certain values to be true, even if they don't acknowledge or know that they do.

· · ·

Although the topic is no laughing matter, it reminds me of a comedy skit I saw years ago on YouTube. Titled *The Front Fell Off!*, the comedy sketch involves John Clarke and Bryan Dawe debating "the merits of ship design and the concepts of maritime law."[97] In the satirical interview, a senator is questioned by an interviewer about the causes of a shipping mishap and resulting oil spill. Near the end of the sketch, the conversation turns to the environmental effects of the accident:

Interviewer: "So what do you do to protect the environment in cases like this?"
Senator: "Well, the ship was towed outside the environment."
Interviewer: "Into another environment?"
Senator: "No, no, it's been towed *beyond* the environment. … It's not *in* the environment."
Interviewer: "Yeah, but from one environment to another environment?"
Senator: "No, it's *beyond* the environment—it's not *in* an environment. It's *beyond* the environment."

---

97. Practicalboatowner, "The Front Fell Off!," uploaded to YouTube September 8, 2008, https://www.youtube.com/watch?v=8-QNAwUdHUQ.

Interviewer: "Well what's out there?"
Senator: "Nothing's out there!"
Interviewer: "Well, there must be something out there."
Senator: "There is *nothing* out there! All there is is sea, and birds, and fish."
Interviewer: "And?"
Senator: "And 20,000 tons of crude oil."
Interviewer: "And, what else?"
Senator: "And a fire."
Interviewer: "And, anything else?"
Senator: "And the part of the ship that the front fell off. But there's nothing *else* out there."
Interviewer: "Senator Collins, thanks for joining us."
Senator: "It's a complete void …"
Interviewer: "We're out of time."
Senator: "The environment's perfectly safe."

Just like a ship can't be towed to some neutral zone outside the environment, children can't be taught or reared in a value-free or perfectly neutral setting. There simply is no such place. It is impossible for *any* educator, in *any* setting, not to have a worldview, and equally as impossible for them to not let their worldview influence their students. Institutional schools and even homeschools may try to eradicate any sign of values and morals, but the very act of eradicating them is itself a result of a certain belief, namely that education should be "neutral."

The Bigger Picture

So, then, behind the question of religious brainwashing looms much larger matters. These issues are common to all people and permeate all of human history. How you view God, religion, politics, government, and authority will dictate whether you find certain teaching akin to "brainwashing" or not. Depending on your worldview, for example, you'll react differently to the following story.

Brother Andrew, a missionary well known for smuggling Bibles and other resources to persecuted Christians behind the Iron Curtain, tells of a visit he made to a Roman Catholic Church in Yugoslavia in his autobiography, *God's Smuggler*.[98] He was surprised at the lack of young people in the congregation and, to help Brother Andrew understand the reason for this, his guide and interpreter, Nikola, introduced him to a peasant mother whose ten-year-old son, Josif, was not with her at church:

"Tell Brother Andrew why Josif is not here," said Nikola.

"Why is my Josif not with me?" she asked. Her voice was bitter. "Because I am a peasant woman with no education. The teacher tells my son there is no God. The government tells my son there is no God. They say to my Josif, 'Maybe your Mama tells you differently, but we know better, don't we? You must remember that Mama has no education. We will humor her.'"[99]

Andrew goes on to explain that though the Yugoslavian Church, in general, didn't seem to be "under any particular persecution," the closer he looked the more he became "aware of the slow wearing-down process the government was exerting on Christians." He continues saying, "The effort seemed to be centered on the children."

Of course, the Yugoslavian government wasn't the only entity to focus their attention on youth. "He alone, who owns the youth, gains the future," said Hitler in a 1935 speech.[100] Or, if you prefer a less uncomfortable quote, "If your plan is for one year plant rice. If your plan is for ten years plant trees. If your plan is for one hundred years educate children."[101] Throughout all of history, people have rec-

---

98. Brother Andrew, *God's Smuggler* (Bloomington, MN: Chosen Books, 2015).

99. Brother Andrew, *God's Smuggler*, 110.

100. Adolf Hitler, as quoted from a 1935 speech, in "Nazi Conspiracy and Aggression," vol. 1 (Washington, DC: United States Government Printing Office, 1946), 320, http://www.loc.gov/rr/frd/Military_Law/pdf/NT_Nazi_Vol-I.pdf.

101. "Confucius," Goodreads, accessed January 19, 2021, https://www.goodreads.com/quotes/79127-if-your-plan-is-for-one-year-plant-rice-if.

ognized the tremendous impact that child training and education has on the future of humanity.

So where does this leave us? Clearly, there's no easy answer, but we must find ways to move forward despite the ambiguity. For me personally, this means researching and being aware of current and past events so we can learn from it all and avoid repeating history. It means looking under the surface-level banter and getting the deeper picture. It means living out my beliefs and values in an intentional way with as much integrity as possible. If you, like me, believe you'll some day stand before God to give an account of your actions and stewardship during this life, then this also means pressing on towards the goals to which you've been called, despite the voices that would try to deter you.

So What Should Our Motives Be?

There's really no one-size-fits-all answer to what our *specific* goals as educators must be, so it follows that motivations will (and *should*) differ as well. Wikipedia, in its entry for "education," states, "There is no broad consensus as to what education's chief aim or aims are or should be."[102] Of course, we can use placeholder definitions for the sake of conversation like we did in the earlier chapter on effectiveness. We can argue that there *is* a common motivation because we all want to raise kids who are good citizens, intelligent people, and capable, happy adults with jobs. But isn't that just stating the obvious? I've yet to meet someone whose goals for education are to raise *bad* citizens, *unintelligent* people, and *helpless, miserable, un-hirable* adults. So, apart from overgeneralized platitudes and philosophical definitions, what can be said about the goals and motivations of educators? What *should* our motives be?

The answers to this question are many and varied, which brings us to another one of the beauties of homeschooling. Educating at home allows each family the freedom to pursue their own callings

---

102. "Education," Wikipedia, last modified January 11, 2021, https://en.wikipedia.org/wiki/Education.

and goals by following their own unique combination of motivating factors. So if you're considering homeschooling, try to set aside other people's opinions about your decision. Input from others is helpful at times, but at some point you'll need to determine why it is that *your* family should homeschool. And from there, pray for wisdom and discernment to determine whether it's a strong enough motivation to counter any situational obstacles you may have. A few sample scenarios will help illustrate my point.

If your child is in imminent physical or psychological danger at a traditional school, it goes without saying that this is a huge motivating factor. Ensuring their safety is one of your primary jobs as a parent, and this will outweigh virtually any other factor. Uncertainty over the details of teaching methods or even bigger issues, such as how you'll live on one salary, will all take a back seat to the serious motivation to get your kid out of danger. When the red flags are going up, you'll do what needs to be done, whether anyone else thinks your motivation is "good enough" or not.

In other cases, including my own, parents feel God calling them to educate at home. After experiencing unmistakable answers to our prayers for guidance and clarity, we felt that we could do none other than to follow God's leading down this countercultural path. If you find yourself in a similar situation, don't let fear of the unknown stop you. And if God is calling your family to homeschool, know that—whether our secularized culture recognizes it or not—God's calling is a bona fide motive for homeschooling.

Other families have specific academic goals that they feel can better be reached in a highly customizable homeschool setting. A number of families I know started educating at home simply because their three- or four-year-old was already reading and they wanted to keep moving ahead at the child's individual academic pace. The freedom to tailor the pace, schedule, and content of learning is instrumental in helping kids of any ability level to reach their fullest potential.

The list of reasons could go on and on. Off the top of my head I can think of families I know personally who have homeschool motives related to job relocation, missionary work, adoption, faith, special needs, health issues, family bonding, sibling issues, learning disabilities, parent work schedules, child volunteering or career opportunities, and special academic ambitions. Each human is a one-of-a-kind individual, and families are equally as unique. Homeschooling is successful because it's an educational model that can accommodate the diversity of motivations and goals mentioned here plus many more.

So, the question isn't what our motives *should* be but, rather, what they *are*. If you're considering homeschooling, don't worry about what others think your reasons should be or whether they're good enough. Just establish what your reasons are and go from there.

"The Only Thing We Have to Fear ..."[103]

A solid case could be made for most reasons why people decide to homeschool. But I would like to caution new homeschoolers against one particularly slippery, behind-the-scenes motivating factor. Regardless of the reason—whether it's avoiding a threatening public school situation, not wanting to catch any germs, escaping inane testing requirements, or any other intention—if the motivation behind your reason is *fear*, you'll find yourself on the defensive, not really making the most of all that the homeschool lifestyle has to offer.

Early on in our homeschooling journey, a non-homeschooling friend of mine was courageous enough to ask me my true reasons for looking into home education. When I shared positive-focused reasons such as following God's leading for our family and providing a tailored education based on my kids' interests and personalities, she applauded my response and let me know how encouraged she was not to hear fear-based reasons. At the time I was just grateful for a supportive friend, but now, years later, I've realized the wisdom in her feedback.

---

103. Franklin D. Roosevelt, "Inaugural Address," March 4, 1933, as published in Samuel Rosenman, ed., *The Public Papers of Franklin D. Roosevelt, Volume Two: The Year of Crisis, 1933* (New York, NY: Random House, 1938), 11–16.

Homeschooling solely for negative or fear-based reasons is kind of like going on a hot air balloon ride blindfolded. You're still whisked away on an amazing flight. You're still floating freely with great potential for adventure. But with the blindfold on, you'll always be reacting nervously, never able to see the beauty and big-picture possibilities all around you. Fear stifles and stiffens us. Fear makes us retreat inward and sucks the joy out of life. Fear makes a poor motivating factor for home education.

> *Fear makes a poor motivating factor for home education.*

So, if homeschooling truly is the next leg of your family's journey, then step onto that path boldly. Take time to sort out your reasons for homeschooling and word them in a positive way so they can move you towards your goals. For example, don't homeschool just to escape bullies. Instead, do it to encourage positive relationships for your kids. Don't homeschool just to avoid Common Core State Standards. Instead, do it to provide the most effective, custom education possible for your child. Don't homeschool just to evade peer pressure. Instead, do it to instill wholesome values in your kids and strengthen family bonds.

When (not *if*, but *when*) you have a rough homeschooling day in the future, you'll look back at your list of reasons to remind yourself why you're doing this. In that moment, you won't find much comfort in reading a list of fears and things from which you're hiding. What *will* help you is a list of positive, hope-filled goals towards which you're actively working. You'll read reasons that remind you of your calling, and you'll be inspired towards your higher purpose in this endeavor. And the hopefulness and conviction you find in those moments will help you push past frustrations, naysayers, and timidity to finish your race well.

You Can't Weigh "Why"

Some families jump into homeschooling *quickly*, out of necessity, but I can't imagine any of them taking the decision *lightly*. Parents I know who've chosen to homeschool have done their due diligence and then some. In the years leading up to our first year homeschooling, my husband and I had too many late-night discussions to count. We wrote out lists of pros and cons and consulted close friends and family. We read dozens of books and articles, scoured the internet for homeschooling blogs, and sought out podcasts and webinars to learn more. We looked into other educational options and compared them side by side. And we prayed and prayed and prayed.

To those who may still be skeptical of homeschoolers and their intentions, I'd encourage you to find some home educators and start up a conversation. Ask them why they chose the path they did and what their main reasons were. Though you might not make the same decision for your own family, I think you'll find you're talking to someone with valid reasons for the path they've chosen.

And for those of you on the fence about homeschooling your kids, definitely go ahead and get all the information you can. List out your pros and cons. Write down your motivations and reasons for considering it. But know that the blogs and research and books will only take you so far. At some point, you'll likely find the final decision is immeasurable; that is, it can't be weighed on a scale or evaluated on a chart.

It reminds me a bit of trying to decide whether or not to try to have a baby. You might run calculations on whether you can afford to raise a child. You'll probably read books and ask other parents how life will change if you have kids. You might even list out the pros and cons of parenting as best you can guess. But, the moment you add "raise, nurture, and love a new, unique, precious human being" to the "pros" side of the list is when you realize this isn't a decision that can be quantified.

It's similar for homeschooling. You can look at your budget and see how you might make one salary work. You can check into co-ops in your area to make sure you'll have some support and enrichment options. And you're obviously reading books to get an idea of what homeschooling life looks like. But there's a point—when you start to add abstract benefits like "opportunity to instill a love of learning" or "ability to teach to their strengths" to your list of pros—when it becomes clear that motivating factors aren't easy things to weigh.

In time, with much thought and prayer, you will begin to find the reasons for home education that mean the most to you. Your motivation will probably be different than your homeschooling friend's, and that's as it should be. Your reasons might not be acceptable in the eyes of your neighbor or your Aunt Beatrice. That's irritating, but so be it. Your motivation—your "why"—is a unique combination of your own faith, situation, needs, goals, and dreams. Let your reasons spur you on, unhindered, to the great possibilities in store for your family.

12

Community

One of my favorite of Aesop's fables is called *The Man, The Boy, and The Donkey*. To paraphrase, while a man and his son were walking to town with their donkey, they pass by a number of other people who express opinions about the way the family is traveling. When the man, boy, and donkey each walk separately, others tease them for not riding the donkey. So the boy rides the donkey, but then passersby reprimand him for riding while his elderly father walks. In response to that, the father rides and makes the son walk which brings scorn from onlookers since the poor child is made to plod along while his father has it easy. Frustrated, they both mount the donkey which, of course, angers the animal rights activists. Near the end of the story, the father and son end up carrying the donkey, as ridiculous as that is, in an effort to please the people around them. The moral of the story is, if you try to please everyone, you'll end up pleasing no one, not even yourself.[104]

The plight of the man and his son is not unlike the difficulties that homeschooling parents have had trying to walk the counter-cultural path they've chosen. It seems that there's always a bystander ready to share (likely with good intentions) how "that's not the way

---

104. "The Man, the Boy, and the Donkey," Fables of Aesop, May 23, 2020 https://fablesofaesop.com/the-man-the-boy-and-the-donkey.html.

to do it."[105] I've seen this happen most often in regard to the involvement homeschoolers have in their communities.

When a family makes the choice to homeschool, they're sometimes criticized for defecting or sticking their heads in the sand instead of jumping into the fray and doing what they can to help improve the educational system. Home-educating parents are told that running away from problems, such as high-stakes testing or violence in schools, won't help solve them. Some onlookers remind homeschoolers that we all need to work together, for the sake of all children, to ensure that a positive educational experience is available to everyone.

So, in response to this pressure, perhaps the prospective homeschooling parents reconsider. They decide to keep their child in public school and be as involved as they can be in the traditional school system, working for positive changes and giving their input to do their part. But they soon find, as several of my teacher and public school parent friends have shared with me, that their power to revamp the system is limited. Teachers and parents who try to promote change are often scolded for rocking the boat, being divisive, or not being team players.

But the other option—to stay in the school system and *not* try to help improve it and to squelch your ideas and comply for the sake of conformity—is analogous to the man and boy carrying the donkey. It's not helping anyone, and it's likely the most inadvisable of all the options. The school system is not improved, your ideas are not heard, your resentment will build, and your own children will be caught in the middle of it all. What's a parent to do?

Some would say homeschooling is the answer for all. Others maintain that public or private school for everyone is the solution. I believe that none of these extremes account for the uniqueness of individuals, families, and situations represented by humankind. Therefore, parents should do whatever they've determined, through much

---

105. S. Lewis, *One-Minute Bedtime Stories* (New York, NY: Doubleday Books for Young Readers, 1982), 10–11.

prayer and careful deliberation, to be the correct decision for *their family*, without worrying about what the onlookers and passersby might say to deter them. This is easier said than done, I know. But still, it's the best way to live out your values. It's the best way to effect positive change in your circles of influence, whatever those circles might be. It's the best way to help your own children, and it's the best way to directly and indirectly serve your community.

Homeschoolers in the Community

There are many ideas of what healthy community looks like and what supporting that community entails. Some researchers and sociologists who study this type of thing focus their work on the physical spaces (parks, green space, infrastructure, etc.) that differentiate thriving communities from less desirable areas. Others study the institutions and programs or offerings that attract people to a neighborhood (e.g., schools, libraries, park districts, and technology). Still others analyze the impact of governance, regulations, and involvement of citizens to better understand what makes communities succeed. Research is also done to explore less tangible elements of society such as feelings of safety, connectedness, or openness that make people feel welcome and comfortable in a community. Suffice it to say, this is another vast, hard-to-define topic.

Here, yet again, we see how a proper understanding of homeschooling opportunities and effectiveness will color your opinion on whether homeschoolers are doing their part for their neighborhoods and our society as a whole. If, in your mind, home-educating families are hermits in their basements, then it's hard to imagine how they'd be making much of an impact on their communities in any of the ways listed above. If you feel that their teaching is ineffective, it's difficult to see how the kids would reach their full potential which, in turn, means we've lost out on that child's gifts and contributions to our world.

As I've hopefully made clear by now, though, opportunity and effectiveness are actually *benefits* of homeschooling, not hindrances. The interplay between homeschoolers and their communities is one of the primary places we see these benefits play out. Home educa-tion's innumerable opportunities for social interaction and self-ac-tualization, and its successful personalized method of instruction, positively impact our world in both the short and long terms in a variety of ways.

Opportunity and effectiveness are actually benefits *of homeschooling, not hindrances.*

Positive Traits, Positive Impact

Like I said, it's difficult to make generalizations about homeschoolers. But, as we saw earlier, they do typically have important *reasons* for their decision, and they share the prerequisite traits of *resourcefulness* and *responsibility*. While specific, individual metrics may vary widely, it's also safe to say the group, as a whole, tends to be dedicated and engaged. Homeschoolers must embody these traits to some degree to even begin their homeschooling journey and certainly to continue it successfully for any length of time. Without dedication to their cause, parents would never muster enough courage to step out of the cultural tide and stay their unique course. And, by definition, they are engaged in the education of their kids, wearing as many hats as needed to get the job done.

If you asked any mayor or community leader what qualities they'd like to see in their citizens and community volunteers, I'd bet that topping their list would be at least a few of the traits in the last paragraph. Engaged, dedicated, responsible, intentional, and resourceful: these are key characteristics needed in individuals and groups trying to build and maintain healthy communities.

Throughout the rest of this chapter, you'll see how, at each level—individual, family, local sub-communities, and the larger so-ciety—homeschoolers can and do impact their circles of influence in positive ways by living out these key traits and their own values. Homeschooling is a boon for any society. Institutions and neighborhoods benefit when they find ways to cooperate with and support homeschoolers in mutually beneficial partnerships.

Sphere of Influence #1: Self

Communities are made up of people. The more emotionally intelligent, responsible, and vocationally satisfied people are involved in a community, the better off it will be. In other words, healthy, thriving individuals lead to healthy, thriving communities. So, it follows then that one of the fundamental ways to positively impact our com-

> *Homeschooling is a boon for any society. Institutions and neighborhoods benefit when they find ways to cooperate with and support homeschoolers in mutually beneficial partnerships.*

munities is to improve and mature as individuals. Any stride taken towards the emotional, physical, intellectual, spiritual, and relational health of any individual has a multiplied effect as that person interacts with hundreds of other people over the course of their life. This ripple effect impacts all the communities touched by that individual. Just ask George Bailey in the classic movie *It's a Wonderful Life*.[106]

Parents who decide to homeschool do so because they have reason to believe that their child's whole personhood will be positively affected by the decision. They know their child better than anyone else does and they know, or are willing to figure out, the most effec-

---

106. *It's a Wonderful Life*, directed by Frank Capra (California, USA: Liberty Films, 1946), DVD.

tive ways to reach that child. Homeschooling is unmatched in its ability to enable individualized, tailored instruction for each student. Because of the freedom parents have in customizing their home-school methods and content, they can teach to the *student*—the *whole* student—instead of teaching to the test or to generic content standards.

Academically, being able to choose, say, a fifth-grade math book and a first-grade writing curriculum for your eight-year-old allows him to proceed with success in both subjects, building not just knowledge but confidence along the way. Emotionally, any character problems that pop up won't fall through the cracks as easily in a class of three as they would in a class of twenty-three. Parents can be quick to see and act, taking as long as needed to work on heart issues such as honesty, compassion, and perseverance. Physically, families can set specific goals for their health and exercise, beyond what we usually think of P.E. class encompassing, knowing they'll have more time and freedom to achieve them.

_____ • • •

Homeschooling is, at a fundamental level, an apprenticeship in life.

_____ • • •

Abeles, quoted earlier, says that "downtime is a catalyst for self-discovery and autonomy."[107] The efficiency and freedom of home-schooling gives students this opportunity regularly. For the youngest homeschoolers, this means more time for self-directed play and natural learning to unfold. With more time, older students can hone life and job skills to achieve higher levels of autonomy sooner than would otherwise be possible.

---

107. Abeles and Rubenstein, *Beyond Measure*, 63.

Homeschooling is, at a fundamental level, an apprenticeship in life. As homeschooled students journey through their K–12 years, most of them can't help but soak in a self-directed, motivated, autonomous manner of being—if not because of their parents' direct instruction in how to be a grown-up, then at least as firsthand witnesses of their parents' efforts. By the time homeschooled kids are launching out on their own, they're ready to jump in as active, engaged community members, giving more than they take. Their "apprenticeship" experience was so closely aligned with the requirements of adult life, they are well prepared to positively impact their community.

Sphere of Influence #2: Family

Strong families are the building blocks of healthy communities. This is why it's so devastating when families break down. The effects are much further-reaching than just the individuals involved, disrupting lives both outwardly throughout the community and forward into future generations. Functional families, on the other hand, do the opposite. They can bless and improve their neighborhoods, help support other individuals, and leave a positive legacy for future generations.

Now, I'm not claiming that homeschooling families are perfect or that you have to homeschool for your family to be an influence for good in your neighborhood. Functional families come in all educational stripes. In fact, as writer and speaker Danielle Strickland once said, a "utopian idea is an enemy of a practical reality."[108] She was talking about how the desire to find the *perfect* church community precludes us from ever finding the true community for which we're looking, but the same applies to families as well. The desire to be a "model family" and the idea that homeschoolers (or any other group) are "perfect families" are both deceptions. There are no such things. And expecting the impossible from an educational method, or striving constantly to achieve an unattainable level of perfection,

---

108. Danielle Strickland, "Willow Creek Community Church Sermon," April 29, 2018, South Barrington, IL.

will only keep us from reaching our fullest potential as thriving (but not perfect) families.

Non-homeschoolers wonder, though, how surrounding yourself with your kids every waking moment of every single day could possibly lead to anything but insanity and family disintegration: the exact opposite of thriving. As I mentioned earlier, the "with your kids 24/7" stereotype isn't true; in reality, you're free to create your own balance of togetherness and separation. Drop-off co-ops, trading childcare, extracurricular classes, date nights and weekend getaways, mom's nights out, nap times, and daily quiet times are just a handful of ways to help find that balance. But, since the default location in homeschooling is home (in other words, since you're together unless you've intentionally planned *not* to be), homeschooling families are often with each other considerably more than their non-homeschooling counterparts.

There is a transition period for families stepping out of the traditional school system or leaving the workforce to stay home. In homeschool circles, this is know as "deschooling" (a season of relaxed expectations) and is usually recommended, allowing everyone a chance to adjust to their new normal. After this transition, or after a family has been homeschooling for a little while, they often find that increased family bonding has promoted healthy changes in themselves and their kids. As Kim John Payne, MEd, writes in *Simplicity Parenting*, "Our instincts strengthen with regular moments of connection with our kids; we're more responsive, less reactive. We can become a better judge of when there is cause for concern. Our hair trigger relaxes."[109]

Homeschooling doesn't magically create perfect families and obedient children. If your kids don't listen to you when you tell them to clean their room, they won't listen to you when you try to teach math either. But that doesn't preclude someone from educating at home. In fact, it might be a good reason to start! Homeschooling

---

109. Kim John Payne, *Simplicity Parenting: Using the Extraordinary Power of Less to Raise Calmer, Happier, and More Secure Kids* (New York, NY: Ballantine Books, 2010), 216.

gives families the extra time and space to work through those relational and character issues more regularly and thoroughly than they would be able to otherwise.

Also, homeschooling typically ensures that siblings aren't strangers to each other. Instead, their schedules and often even academic learning can be aligned, strengthening their relationship and sense of connection. When my two oldest kids were about seven and five, I gave them a fun end-of-school-year survey. It had been an exciting year, full of interesting outings, enjoyable learning activities, and new friendships, so I was sure I'd see "LEGOLAND" or "the chocolate factory field trip" or "playing outside on Mud Day" (it's what it sounds like) on their papers. But much to my surprise and delight, under "favorite memory from this year" my oldest had written "I love my brother!!!" That made it all worth it. Even Mud Day.

Beyond sibling and parent relationships, homeschooling can bolster connections with extended family members, too. Without the time and schedule restrictions of traditional schooling, visits with grandparents, aunts, and uncles—whether locally or farther away—can happen more regularly. My kids' grandparents frequently join us, not just at band concerts and sporting events, but for field trips during school hours and special academic project days. Some homeschoolers I know even outsource entire subjects to experienced grandparents and other relatives. What an amazing opportunity to be instructed weekly in woodworking under your grandfather, a master carpenter with over forty years of training and knowledge. What a unique experience to spend a week every quarter at your aunt and uncle's dairy farm or to shadow your cousin in his entrepreneurial venture for days at a time.

Just imagine the compounding benefits of this kind of symbiotic, natural learning, not just squeezed in during already overfilled summer breaks, but all year round! For one, parents get a break, plus free private tutoring for their kids. Students get amazing, hands-on, apprenticeship-style learning experiences from experts who love them dearly. And the extended family members are able to share years of accumulated knowledge and experience while enjoying time with their family, creating an incredible, lasting legacy. Home education fosters the kind of lifelong family bonds and feelings of belonging that will strengthen and support families, and therefore communities, for generations to come.

Home education fosters the kind of lifelong family bonds and feelings of belonging that will strengthen and support families, and therefore communities, for generations to come.

Sphere of Influence #3: Local Communities

Jim Mason, VP of litigation for HSLDA, recalls a time he spoke at a Leadership Conference sponsored by the Home Educators Association of Virginia. The attendees represented a wide variety of homeschooling families, groups, and associations. "Those associations," he writes, "were big and small, local and statewide, led by rookies and by veterans, diverse in makeup but united in purpose—providing a quality educational and social experience for their own children, their friends' children, and their communities' children. Drawn by this common goal, they cheerfully gathered together on that fine spring morning to learn how to do it better. And no statute, regulation, or state official required them to be there or paid their way."[110]

Humanity was created for connection. Since the modern form of this grassroots movement began, home educators have been creating little pockets of support and camaraderie everywhere they go. Whether at educational conferences, weekly co-ops, or backyard

---

110. Jim Mason, "The Civic Virtue of Private Home Education," *The Home School Court Report* (4th Quarter 2018), accessed March 8, 2021, from https://read.nxtbook.com/hslda/the_home_school_court_report/fourth_quarter_2018_vol34_no4/the_civic_virtue_of_private_h.html.

playdates, home educators naturally pursue and thrive on community. When new homeschoolers meet each other, one of the first questions they ask is, "Which co-op are you in?" There's no question that homeschooling families support and encourage each other within their local homeschooling groups.

What's astonishing to me, though, is the misguided notion that home educators are somehow crippling their local communities through their lack of involvement. This couldn't be further from the truth. Homeschoolers, as individuals and as groups, are out in their local neighborhoods, interacting with and supporting their communities on a daily basis.

They bring laughter to neighborhood playgrounds, soccer fields, and walking paths which are otherwise void of occupants younger than twenty during school hours. Socializing with each other and the neighbors they find there, homeschoolers' outdoor recreation is a very visible part of their community involvement. They also create enough collective demand for weekday daytime classes that park districts are now adding "homeschool" sections in their course catalogs. Both village-owned and privately owned fitness, pool, music, art, dance, roller-skating, and theater facilities—once underutilized on weekdays—are now supported by the growing homeschool demographic looking to round out their children's elective courses.

I've had grateful staff members at libraries and children's museums actually thank me for giving them an opportunity to do their job! Educators in these facilities are *longing* for ways to reach more students. They *want* to share their expertise and their resources. Do you want to help support those educators? Bring them a small number of students during a slow time of day and give them more time than usual to connect with the kids—they'll be thrilled! Local tutors, private instructors, and retired teachers are also able to fill their daytime hours teaching co-op classes or individual homeschooled students in foreign language, gym, karate, music lessons, and more.

Home-educating families are also regularly supporting local companies, not just during evenings and weekends like their public-schooled peers but also during weekday daytime hours. Where do homeschoolers stop for lunch on the way back from their two-hour volunteering shift? Where do my kids and I get snacks after our trips to the library? Where do homeschooled teens meet for their morning book club? At their local businesses, that's where. Besides the obvious financial benefit, this has a stabilizing effect on the rush-hour patterns the traditional school system has on local establishments. It also helps re-balance the age segregation our communities experience during school hours.

Whether through frequent field trips, household errands, co-op outings, or volunteering, homeschoolers are often out interacting with their neighbors. Not being confined to a school building, they are free to engage with their local communities in a variety of ways on a daily basis.

Sphere of Influence #4: Larger Society and Culture

The impacts made in these spheres of influence have a compounding and circular effect. Homeschooling produces healthy, well-educated individuals and also promotes thriving families. Intentional, engaged families tend to produce healthy, well-educated students. Flourishing families and individuals are more likely to build up and support their communities which causes communities, composed of these healthy family units, to be more effective at supporting other members of the community. Having stronger networks of support helps those other families and individuals to thrive, and the cycle continues. And when we look past the borders of our towns to our states, country, and world, this web of positive impact grows exponentially.

In addition to this somewhat indirect, trickle-down influence, there are many other specific areas in which homeschoolers impact our culture and larger society in beneficial ways. For one, the movement as a whole has contributed to an explosion of alternative curriculum resources that have benefitted both homeschoolers and non-homeschoolers alike.

Demme Learning, for instance, is a company birthed out of a homeschool co-op math class, taught by home educator and former schoolteacher Steve Demme, in the late 1980s. The success of his classes led him to formalize and begin selling his curriculum, Math-U-See, to homeschooling families. Years later, the company's reach expanded to serve in intervention and special education settings outside the homeschool community. "Success in [those programs] led to expansion into schools and small classroom environments."[111] Today, the next generation of the Demme family has picked up the torch, as the company continues to grow and support education worldwide.

Students everywhere are the main beneficiaries when parents (both home educators and not), classroom teachers, tutors, and educators of all kinds work *together* and share resources. A diversity of ideas—looking at education from all different angles—gives educators the best chance to reach each child in their care. Homeschoolers, and the many thousands of curricula, companies, podcasts, books, and blogs born out of the movement, bring unique perspectives and resources to the table. They've both benefitted from, and been a benefit to, the big-picture educational community.

Similarly, homeschoolers' civic involvement is profitable for their own education and also for our society. "Appropriate education … makes children aware of important cultural values and provides skills enabling children to participate productively in their communities and the larger society through various forms of civic engagement."[112] When she wrote this, Elizabeth Bartholet, the Harvard Law professor who later calls for a "presumptive ban" on homeschooling in the same article, meant this statement as a criticism of homeschooling. Because homeschooling, in her view, isn't an "appropriate" form of education, she concludes that home educators are "not likely to be capable of satisfying the democratic function [of education]." Ironically, though, her quote above clearly outlines exactly what many homeschools *do* provide their kids.

Take the Illinois Christian Home Educators (ICHE) Legislative Days annual event in Springfield, Illinois, for example. Scores

111. "History of Math-U-See," Math-U-See, accessed January 21, 2021, https://www.mathusee.com/parents/about/history-of-math-u-see/.

112. Elizabeth Bartholet, "Homeschooling: Parent Rights Absolutism vs. Child Rights to Education and Protection," *Arizona Law Review* 62, no. 1 (2019): 4, https://arizonalawreview.org/pdf/62-1/62arizlrev1.pdf.

of homeschooling students and parents gather in the state capitol to pray for the leaders of our state and nation, learn about civil government, and distribute hundreds of cherry pies to our state's lawmakers and their staff. Executive Director of ICHE Kirk Smith explains, "We want to be part of the political process. It's one thing to read about it in books, but it's another thing to experience it first hand. To walk the same corridors of power wherein laws are made … not just talking about history but being an actual part [of it]."[113]

One popular online homeschool curriculum store, Rainbow Resource Center,[114] offers over 450 governmental, political, and civic resources. And this doesn't include the government lessons you'd find in many of their other history and literature offerings. Homeschooling parents certainly have no shortage of resources to teach their kids about civics. And if the products weren't selling, the store wouldn't be offering them.

As for learning about cultural values and engaging with our larger world, homeschoolers have more time and freedom than most to travel, and many take full advantage of the opportunity! Families plan trips to align with their studies, traveling to the Liberty Bell and Constitution Hall to "supplement American history lessons," for example.[115] Or, they simply take advantage of teachable moments on their family vacations. Some even make travel a feature of their education, taking their schools on the road in their RV or, rather, making the *world* their school.[116] Homeschool travel groups, like Traveling Homeschoolers,[117] are another option for larger, life-changing travel experiences. There's really no substitute for firsthand experiences.

I think Mark Twain would agree. In *Innocents Abroad*, he famously writes, "Travel is fatal to prejudice, bigotry, and narrow-

113. Illinois Christian Home Educators, "Legislative Days," uploaded to YouTube May 15, 2017, https://www.youtube.com/watch?time_continue=64&v=oHuGSSHoYsl&feature=emb_logo.

114. A website search (keyword: "government"; accessed August 1, 2020, www.rainbowresource.com) provided 476 results for relevant products.

115. Matthew Hennessey, "Homeschooling in the City," *City Journal* (Summer 2015), https://www.city-journal.org/html/homeschooling-city-13742.html.

116. Visit https://wandrlymagazine.com to see some examples of "roadschooling."

117. See https://www.travelinghomeschoolers.com for more information.

mindedness …"[118] Given the opportunity to travel more than they would otherwise have, and being less restricted by the constraints of school hours and semesters, homeschooling families are creating rich, memorable learning experiences for themselves. They're doing *more* than just becoming, to use Bartholet's phrase, "aware of important cultural values." They're sharing their own ideas and supporting other communities as they travel, while at the same time discovering and interacting with the wide-ranging cultures and a rich diversity of perspectives represented worldwide.

Different Is Good

When I was one of the only women in an architecture office full of men, my dissimilar strengths and female perspective contributed to a healthy workspace balance. It benefitted the company to transform its homogenous culture. When I was the only individual at my college job fair who wanted to work in Chicago, it was a win-win for both myself and the firm. When you take a vacation and break free of your daily ruts, it gives you a fresh outlook on life. Different is often a good thing.

It took me a long time to open my mind up to the idea that learning and teaching can happen in ways other than those I experienced in my own public-school upbringing. In fact, I still find myself defaulting back to ideas such as tests, siloed subjects, and textbook lesson plans since those methods are so ingrained in my own experience and our culture. If you're raised in a certain system—a certain way of thinking—it can be very hard to step outside of it to see other ways of doing things.

It reminds me of a season in high school when I tutored a grade school boy in math. As his tutor, I often found presenting the material in a new way or from a different angle helped him have a light-

---

118. Mark Twain, *Innocents Abroad* (HTML version, public domain), conclusion, released June 22, 2004, http://www.gutenberg.org/ebooks/3176.

bulb moment. If he was stuck on a topic, presenting the material in the same way over and over just didn't help. It took a new perspective to move him forward.

Homeschooled kids are growing up with a different perspective than the vast majority of their peers. Some home educators might still use tests, lesson plans, and textbooks as part of their repertoire, but, overall, each homeschooling family is developing their own *unique* approach to education. As these kids grow up and join the workforce as teachers, leaders, parents, bosses, and employees, their unique perspectives—their "different angles" on how humanity can educate, learn, and develop—will be invaluable. Homeschoolers are already living an "outside-the-box" lifestyle, so it's not a stretch for them to think that way naturally.

Lori Pickert, author of *Project-Based Homeschooling: Mentoring Self-Directed Learners*, describes another advantageous outcome of this "different" upbringing. "The point of project-based [interest-led, experience-based] homeschooling isn't only to become a skilled thinker and learner. It's just as important to find out what you're good at and what inspires you to work your hardest—so you can *do as much of it as possible*"[119] (emphasis mine). More students free to deeply explore and practice their individual life purpose means more satisfied workers sharing a wider variety of gifts and talents with their communities. As school choice advocate Hayden K. Smith writes, "… the nation needs to come to terms with the fact that mandatory public education simply isn't the only, or even the best, option for the public welfare."[120]

Separatists? I Don't Think So

If you'll recall the early chapters of this book, I shared how before we started homeschooling, I thought homeschoolers were part of a "paral-

119. Lori Pickert, *Project-Based Homeschooling: Mentoring Self-Directed Learners* (Scotts Valley, CA: CreateSpace, 2012), 142.

120. Hayden K. Smith, "A Brief History of Public Education: School Choice in America Part II," FreedomWorks, February 13, 2013, http://www.freedomworks.org/content/brief-history-public-education-school-choice-america-part-ii.

lel universe"—separate and distinct, doing their own thing. Although I personally thought of this in a neutral way, the idea that homeschooling "breeds separatism"[121] is a criticism some still use to defend their stance against home education. Now, though, I see that my initial picture was ill informed. Homeschoolers are people who've made an intentional choice to do life and education in a certain way for a variety of reasons. Although their schedules or routines may be different from the majority, they're no more "separate" than any other group with specific life goals that might differentiate them from the norm.

For example, night-shift workers aren't hiding from society; they just have a less common work schedule. Firefighters sleep and eat at their stations for days at a time but, of course, no one would make the claim that they're "separatists." Entrepreneurs and those who work from home aren't part of some parallel, isolated society even though they are often their own bosses, creating their own schedules and structuring their own time differently than others. In fact, the work all these people are doing greatly benefits our communities and they are able to have a greater impact *because* of the very differences that distinguish them from the majority. Just like homeschoolers, they are people—families and individuals—who have a calling or goal to achieve and who are prepared to let their finances, time, resources, and routines run against the cultural current to stay true to their purpose.

As we've seen, home education provides an excellent way for kids and parents to interact with—and positively impact—every level of their communities. Starting at the individual level and radiating out through their larger concentric spheres of influence, homeschooled students and their parents are contributing to our world in countless ways. As the homeschooling movement continues to grow, the greatest positive impact will be seen in communities whose members—no matter their method of educating—find ways to share resources, build relationships, and focus on common goals for the educational benefit of *all* their students and citizens of *all* ages.

121. "Home Schooling Should Be Banned," Debate-Wise, accessed January 21, 2021, https://debate-wise.org/debates/2256-home-schooling-should-be-banned/.

13

This Is the (Homeschooling) Life

At times I've wondered how it's possible for me to have started with such a narrow, inaccurate view of homeschooling and, within just a few years, to have ended up where I am now. But, looking back, it's really not a mystery. It was a matter of clarifying misunderstandings and opening my mind and heart to new information and experiences. My own journey essentially followed the path laid out in the chapters of this book.

Once I understood that the social and academic opportunities are many and varied for homeschoolers, and after I grasped just how effective home education can be, there was no question in my mind that I had stumbled across a potentially amazing option for our family. After researching more about how families make homeschooling a practical reality and getting our feet wet by starting our own homeschool adventure, it became clear that this really could work for us. Through prayer, discussion, and practice, my husband and I solidified our motives and mission and began to really find our footing. The amazing relationships we found within our homeschooling groups, as well as the positive impact I witnessed homeschoolers having on their larger surrounding communities, all served to reinforce my belief that this educational method is a beneficial alternative for numerous families and our society as a whole.

So far, in this book, we've talked through the five aspects of homeschooling that tend to cause confusion or are misunderstood.

Homeschoolers often find themselves on the defensive, having to explain how they socialize or how they'll manage to teach calculus to their son ten years in the future. In reality, though, the biggest purported drawbacks to homeschooling—that is, the areas most questioned by non-homeschoolers—are actually the *main advantages* to the method.

— · · ·

The biggest purported drawbacks to homeschooling–that is, the areas most questioned by non-homeschoolers–are actually the main advantages *to the method.*

— · · ·

Far from being a hindrance to socialization, homeschooling can actually provide *more* unique, meaningful social opportunities in a wider variety of contexts and settings than are available to students bound by traditional school schedules and facilities. Not only is homeschooling *not in*effective, the tailored education possible with home instruction is repeatedly shown to often be *more* effective than other options. As for practicality, though admittedly countercultural, the homeschooling lifestyle can be even *more* practical than public or private schooling for many families, allowing them to pursue family togetherness, entrepreneurship, mission work, travel, and any number of other unique group or individual callings. And, while their motives might be questioned, homeschooling families, by and large, are pursuing the path they know is best for the health, welfare, and education of their own children. In doing so, they are working, along with all other educators, towards the betterment of our communities, both now and in the future.

But, as I've repeatedly stated, every homeschool is unique. Each family has their own goals, needs, and priorities. This means that even the general descriptions of the last paragraph will apply in different ways to different homeschools. This can make it difficult, especially for outsiders, to determine whether or how homeschooling is working for a specific homeschooler they've met or to decide how well homeschooling might work for their own family.

To better understand how homeschooling really works, we need to switch gears. So far, we've been clarifying and rebutting specific misconceptions. We'll now shift away from this focus and summarize the big-picture reasons why homeschooling is successful. Instead of explaining what homeschooling is *not*, this last chapter will cover the overarching beneficial features of homeschooling—that is, what it *is*—and why it works for so well for so many unique families and situations.

Ultimately, there are three major assets that all homeschools possess, regardless of the family's motives, location, teaching styles, resources, or goals. These three features are intrinsically intertwined but are each a distinct advantage. Collectively, they are the reason homeschooling is so successful for families from all walks of life. The key benefits of home-based education are *freedom*, *time*, and *wellness*.

---

* * *

The key benefits of home-based education are freedom, time, and wellness.

* * *

Free as a Bird

I would like to make one clarification before we continue. When I talk about freedom, I do not mean "license to do anything." Parents exercising the freedoms enabled by homeschooling are no more permitted to engage in illegal activity than anyone else. So, just to be unmistakably clear, "freedom" in this book means freedom within the bounds of already existing laws and regulations that govern our free society.

You've already seen the recurrent concept of freedom woven throughout the previous chapters. Each year we homeschool, I realize more and more how the idea of freedom isn't just a theme that shows up from time to time. It is *the* theme. Freedom is the principal, foundational characteristic of home education from which all of its other merits flow. Without it, the other benefits of homeschooling cannot be realized. Putting it another way, to the extent freedom is stifled, so too will the advantages of homeschooling be hindered. If the homeschooling lifestyle—with its bounty of opportunities and potential advantages—is a treasure chest, then freedom is the key to that chest.

At first, it wasn't easy for me to grasp just how much freedom homeschoolers really have. In fact, we were several years into this adventure before I really began to understand just how unencumbered we were. Even now, I still find myself recognizing areas in which our potential has been stifled simply because I never really thought about doing it another way. It's just too easy to be pulled along by the cultural flow, or your own daily routines, without stopping to think about alternatives. But if you step out of the current long enough to consider your options, you'll often find that even small customizations go a long way to improve productivity and satisfaction.

As books like *Creative Schools*[122] substantiate, the more teachers are allowed to tailor the curricula, activities, schedules, and routines to their unique students and situation, the more gains are made. I recall a grade school teacher of mine allowing children in our small, five-student, gifted math breakout group to stand on chairs when completing math problems on the chalkboard and leap off dramatically when finished. I'm sure this slightly chaotic (and somewhat dangerous) practice wouldn't have been approved by her superiors, but she was a wise teacher, attuned to the needs of her students. She knew some kinetic activity would help take the edge off the difficult math assignments for our little group of anxiety-prone, perfectionistic, active learners. We loved the class and even looked forward to

---

122. Robinson, *Creative Schools*.

learning math and tackling hard problems. I have no doubt that those unique experiences, which were the result of an educator exercising her freedom, helped shape my favorable view of math and planted the first seeds of the engineering path I later pursued.

Now imagine this on a more comprehensive scale. No, I don't mean to picture hundreds of students flailing around as they leap off of chairs. I mean picture a parent who loves their child immensely and knows their child's personality, needs, and strengths in great detail. Picture that parent having the ability not just to allow chair jumping as a reward for correct answers in fourth-grade math class but to develop a *customized* educational plan for that student in *each* subject for *every* year. The impact of an individualized education like this can hardly be overstated. Homeschoolers are as free as birds, and it's this freedom which allows them to soar.

Free to Be Us

If you haven't homeschooled, it can be hard to visualize the ways this freedom might play out in day-to-day reality. One of the things that most helped me understand what it is homeschoolers do all day was reading "A Day in the Life ..." blog posts[123] in which homeschooling parents share pictures and descriptions of an average day in their homeschool. It's through reading these posts that I really began to see how limiting my prior views were. And I don't mean just my views of education. There were *so many* aspects of life—career paths, schooling, schedules, health, and wellness—in which I'd just been blindly following the societal crowd.

The autobiographical blog posts of homeschooling families were shocking to me at first because they often made me question some of these major life areas I thought I had already figured out. I thought I knew the "proper procedure" for raising a family in America in the twenty-first century, but these homeschool bloggers were opening my eyes to entirely different ways of doing life.

---

123. To read about a typical day in my own homeschool, visit https://www.sensiblehomeschool.com/a-day-in-the-life-of-a-homeschool-family/.

Since then, I've seen firsthand just how many aspects of life are impacted where more freedom exists. The following anecdotes from my own family's experience provide just a few concrete examples of how foundational freedom is to effectiveness.

Freedom in Priorities

Over the years, our family has been able to align our life with our priorities in ways I never thought possible. For example, intergenerational family time has always been especially important to us. Our choice to homeschool allowed my two oldest kids to spend, I'd estimate, at least ten times the hours with my mother-in-law than they would have otherwise been able to since we incorporated regular "Grandma visits" during traditional school hours. When she passed away of pancreatic cancer in 2016, I was incredibly grateful for the memories and experiences our flexible schedule had allowed us to enjoy with her. Those extra visits were priceless.

Freedom of Methods

Homeschooling has allowed us to use whatever methods of learning are most helpful for each of my kids. Neither they nor I have ever been too keen on worksheets or textbooks, so I knew those methods wouldn't work for us. Notebooking, however, which is a kind of freestyle, academic journaling, has helped my kids retain information effectively because they write and draw about the aspects of our science and history studies that pique their interest. This type of individualized approach is often tricky to use in classroom settings since the work produced is difficult to compare and grade. I'm regularly amazed at the information my kids have retained due to our ability to experiment with new methods and use what works best for each child.

Freedom of Content

While planning language arts for my then early elementary–aged kids, I found there to be great redundancy in grammar curricula. I agreed with grammar experts, such as Robin Finley, author of *Analytical Grammar*,[124] and others that there's no reason to repeat the same basic grammar lessons year after year. A noun is a noun. By consolidating lessons and choosing efficient, mastery-based curricula, we've saved time and spared ourselves unnecessary, boring repetition in this relatively finite subject. Consequently, we've had more time to add in extra logic and critical thinking activities that our family enjoys and finds important.

Freedom from Red Tape

Most homeschoolers are free from much of "the system" that bogs public and even private schools down. If a change is needed, parents can turn on a dime to correct a problem. Early in my oldest son's fifth-grade year, it was clear that the plans I'd made for math would need to be revamped. The instructional method and type of assignments that had worked when he was younger seemed to be stifling his growing interest in higher math concepts. My son and I talked about the situation, the pros and cons of his current curriculum, and what we'd both like to see changed. We researched together and tried sample lessons of other math programs. Over the course of *one weekend*, we found a new, high-quality program that he began using that Monday. The decision-making power remained in the hands of the ones directly impacted by the decision, with zero time wasted on countless committee meetings and bureaucracy.

Inside the Treasure Chest

If freedom is the key to unlocking the treasure chest of homeschooling advantages, then the remaining two central benefits, time and wellness, are the shiny treasures waiting within. In fact, you can think of time and wellness as two sides of the same valuable coin. We can use our time to become well by, say, getting proper sleep,

---

124. For more information about the *Analytical Grammar* curriculum, visit https://www.analytical-grammar.com.

preparing home-cooked meals, or exercising. But, it's also true that the healthier we are (in the broadest sense of the term *healthy*), the more effectively we can *use* our time. For example, if I'm sick with the flu, then I am not able to use my gifts and abilities to help others. Instead, my time is being used to rest and recuperate. The more I can make progress towards mental, spiritual, and physical wellness, the more I can use my time to give back to others and work towards family or societal goals.

Let's talk about the time side of the treasure coin first. But, as we do, keep in mind that the freedom to adjust one's daily schedule—to sleep in an hour later or take a break when you need to—is just the tip of the iceberg. With more authority over their own time, homeschoolers might choose to study one subject in depth each day, schedule less each day but work through the summer, take off all of December, travel abroad during the "school year"—the ideas are limitless. Generally speaking, they have more free time to work with and more control over how that time is used at both small and large scales.

Hidden Costs

You may remember learning about the concept of opportunity cost in a high school or college economics class. If you need a quick refresher, this idea is the reason that once you buy an overpriced, Chicago-style hot dog at a ballgame for $8, you can't use that same $8 to buy raffle tickets. People and matter can't be two places at the same time (unless you're a quantum physicist, in which case I'd like to hear your ideas on how I can improve my productivity). So then, the hidden cost of making one choice is the *inability* to choose something else.

This is true in terms not only of money but of people and time as well. If I choose to go to the park with my kids for the afternoon, I can't also do my grocery shopping during that same time frame. If you're like me, you might try to cheat the system by "multitasking" or rushing around like a headless chicken, but the truth remains that we cannot be in two places at once.

Therefore, each choice we make *for* one thing is a choice *against* everything else in that moment. We saw this earlier in the discussion concerning homeschool socialization. Each moment in a classroom is a moment *not* spent talking with neighbors and vice versa. This is one example, but the entire discussion of which educational method to pursue revolves around the concept of opportunity cost. Basically it comes down to how you want to spend your time. What are the things you want to *choose* to include in your life and your kids' lives even though it means foregoing the seemingly infinite number of other options?

Time Flies

The decision to homeschool greatly impacts your ability to manage your own time. If we do a quick calculation,[125] we find that public-schooled students spend approximately 1,213 hours per year in school. Over the course of a K–12 education, this adds up to over 15,700 hours of their lives, *not including commuting time and homework.* Imagine being able to gain back more than 15,700 hours of your children's lives and using those hours to provide a unique combination of personalized instruction based on your family's goals and your children's specific needs. As Carl Sandburg once said, "Time is the coin of your life. It is the only coin you have, and only you can determine how it will be spent. Be careful lest you let other people spend it for you."[126]

From the single moments in each day to entire years, homeschooling families are taking back the time that is theirs to steward here on this Earth. We might not be able to precisely quantify the impact of the ability to customize your schedule, but a quick conver-

---

125. The U.S. Department of Education, National Center for Education Statistics, Schools and Staffing Survey (SASS), *Public School Data File, 2011–12* (accessed January 21, 2021, https://nces.ed.gov/datalab/powerstats/codebook.aspx?dataset=61&type=subject#TOTTIME), states that the average number of hours in the school day in the United States is 6.74 hours. Multiplying 6.74 hours per day by the typical 180 school days per year equates to just over 1,213 hours per year.

126. "Quotation Details," The Quotations Page, accessed January 21, 2021, http://www.quotationspage.com/quote/2989.html.

sation with most any homeschooler will demonstrate that the benefits are considerable and important.

One of my homeschooling friends is grateful for relaxed mornings that now include candlelit, home-cooked breakfasts and Scripture reading as a family instead of toaster pastries gulped down while sprinting out the door. Another family I know schedules their "weekends" on Tuesday and Wednesday to align with the husband's work schedule. It's not an exaggeration to say that they've fostered a deeper relationship with their father by homeschooling.

Ng Chee Meng, former minister of education (schools) in Singapore, once remarked, "We need a better balance in our students' education journey. This means dialing back an excessive focus on academics. We need to *free up time and space* to nurture other dimensions that are just as important for our children's development. Let them not just study the flowers, but also stop to smell the flowers, and wonder at their beauty"[127] (emphasis mine). The efficiency of homeschooling frees up this time.

In the same way it takes me less time to drive straight to the mall in my own car than if I take the city bus, homeschoolers can often finish the academic portion of their day in a fraction of the time classes of twenty or thirty students can. This extra time can be used to "smell the flowers," dig more deeply into topics being studied, or pursue more electives and hobbies than they otherwise could. According to the authors of *Sparks of Genius*, "Recent studies have found that the best predictor of career success in any field is not IQ, grades, or standardized test scores but participation in one or more mentally intensive leisure time activities or hobbies—anything from painting, composing music, or writing poetry to programming computers, creating videos, or playing around with scientific ideas or mathematics."[128]

---

127. Ng Chee Meng, "MOE FY 2016 Committee of Supply Debate" (speech), accessed January 21, 2021, https://www.moe.gov.sg/news/speeches/20160408-moe-fy-2016-committee-of-supply-debate-speech-by-acting-minister-for-education-schools-ng-chee-meng.
128. Root-Bernstein and Root-Bernstein, *Sparks of Genius*, 323.

But authors Sara Bennett and Nancy Kalish ask us, "How will our children know what they want to do, or even what they like, if they don't have the chance [in other words, *time*] to find out?"[129]

Homeschoolers have that time.

Well, Well, Well

The other side of our treasure coin is the incredible opportunity homeschoolers have to promote wellness in their homes. The more any parent is attuned to what's going on in their children's lives, whether academically, physically, or relationally, the better able they are to nurture the student's mind, body, and spirit. The extra time spent with their kids and involvement in their daytime hours allows home educators to guide their student's growth in all of these areas.

Kim John Payne, quoted earlier, warns parents of the war being waged against childhood. "We are building our lives, and our families, on the four pillars of too much: too much stuff, too many choices, too much information, and too much speed."[130] Beyond mere sensory overload, or an occasional feeling of being overwhelmed, Payne alerts us that "such a consistent pattern of stress can accumulate into a PTSD-type [post-traumatic stress disorder] scenario, or CSR [cumulative stress reaction]" for kids.[131] His insightful book outlines steps parents can take to counteract the negative effects of our frenzied "More! Faster! Earlier!"[132] society. "By simplifying, we protect the environment for childhood's slow, essential unfolding of self."[133]

Any parent can utilize the approaches in Payne's book and, in fact, most of his examples were anecdotes from families of traditionally schooled children who saw great improvements after fine-tuning their physical environment, schedules, and routines to match the needs of their children. That said, the freedom of homeschooling removes numerous obstacles that hinder beneficial changes to a

---

129. Bennett and Kalish, *The Case Against Homework*, 26.
130. Payne, *Simplicity Parenting*, 5.
131. Payne, *Simplicity Parenting*, 9.
132. Payne, *Simplicity Parenting*, 217.
133. Payne, *Simplicity Parenting*, 6.

student's learning environment or limit the control they have over their own time. "When your child's best self is more frequently at home, you'll have no trouble protecting their time. You'll instinctively guard the leisure that unfurrows their brow and allows them to follow their curiosity."[134]

In addition to these general positive effects, fewer outside restrictions imposed on homeschooling families means that parents are also able to prioritize and address the needs of their kids in several specific areas:

Physical Wellness

Being home allows parents and kids more time to prepare whole food-based meals and find the eating patterns best for their bodies. Dietary goals are more easily achieved when parents are aware of their kid's food intake. My family, for instance, has been able to keep a closer watch on our blood sugar levels than we'd be able to if our kids weren't with us during the day. Having more consistent control over our snack and meal times has had a stabilizing effect on our mood and overall health. Similarly, students with allergies, especially severe ones, can learn in a safer setting and parents have more time to train them in the management of their particular needs.

Sleep health is another facet of physical wellness that home-based education can improve. Marc Weissbluth, MD, child sleep expert, warns that, for adolescents in particular, there's "not enough time to sleep, especially in the morning."[135] He also reminds us that poor sleep habits established in childhood can negatively affect children into adulthood. "Sleep is a powerful modifier of mood, behavior, performance, and personality."[136] Homeschoolers are free to start school later, eliminate late-night homework sessions, and make other adjustments to their daily routine as needed to align to their kids'

---

134. Payne, *Simplicity Parenting*, 217.
135. Marc Weissbluth, *Healthy Sleep Habits, Happy Child: A Step-by-Step Program for a Good Night's Sleep* (New York, NY: Ballantine Books, 2003), 360.
136. Weissbluth, *Healthy Sleep Habits*, xix.

body rhythms. They can prioritize quality sleeping patterns, which helps them now and sets the stage for optimal sleep health for the rest of their lives.

Movement and physical activity can be integrated in a natural way throughout the day. Not being confined to desks or classrooms, homeschoolers can more easily incorporate large motor activities and exercise breaks. This is beneficial for all students, but particularly those at risk for potential misdiagnoses of behavior disorders and related unwarranted medications. Disabilities and other specific health needs can be monitored and addressed in a more personalized manner as well.

Intellectual Wellness

Home educators are better able than most to take advantage of a student's prime productivity time, especially if their peak learning time doesn't fall within "school hours." Daily and weekly schedules and learning environments can be customized to maximize concentration and provide brain breaks as needed for each individual student. Additional opportunities to work and play outside in nature also contribute to cognitive development and overall health.[137]

Student's freedom to linger over interesting topics and dive more deeply into their academic and hobby work allows them to climb quickly up the levels of Bloom's Taxonomy. This "framework for categorizing educational goals"[138] begins with basic objectives, such as recalling facts, and progresses to more complex mastery of material, such as critique or original design. Free to utilize unconventional methods—engaging in deep Socratic discussions or dropping everything to investigate a topic for hours, for example— homeschoolers can spend much of their time engaged at the top of Bloom's hierarchy.

---

137. Annie Wallin, "Nature Play Is Important for the Cognitive Development of Early Learners," The Center for Advancement of Informal Science Education, February 16, 2017, https://www.informalscience. org/news-views/nature-play-important-cognitive-development-early-learners.

138. "What Is Bloom's Taxonomy?," Bloom's Taxonomy, accessed January 21, 2021, https://www. bloomstaxonomy.net

In home-based settings, families are free to prioritize great litera-ture, music, arts, and other cognitively beneficial electives that might otherwise be squeezed out due to time or financial constraints in tra-ditional classroom settings. Daily opportunities for travel—whether to the grocery store, a museum, or another country—provide train-ing in practical problem solving and life skills as well as stimulation for the imagination.

Emotional Wellness

All of these categories of wellness impact each other, and emotional wellness is no exception. Healthy diet, sleep patterns, and exercise, for example, are all primary factors in nurturing emotional well-being. Having the time and freedom to address those physical needs well gives families a head start towards improving emotional health, too.

Red flags indicating undiagnosed emotional issues are less likely to go unnoticed with low student-to-educator ratios in homes and homeschool co-op settings. And when specific emotional issues, such as chronic stress, depression, or anxiety, are already known, parents are able to keep a closer eye on the situation, ensuring that medica-tions and management protocols set by their doctors and therapists are followed throughout the day.

Homeschooling offers kids a safe space to learn about their feel-ings and develop emotional awareness at a child-friendly pace. They can process events of the day *throughout* the day without the added pressure of peer judgments. And the higher proportion of intergener-ational contact means more opportunities to learn appropriate emo-tional management techniques from adult mentors—people with, perhaps, decades of life experience—rather than same-aged peers.

Spiritual Wellness

The ability for homeschoolers to weave their faith traditions into their school day and learning is a key factor for many who choose home-based education. In my own family, we've enjoyed the free-dom to discuss our beliefs and questions about God and His creation in a very natural way through daily teachable moments. We're grateful for the opportunities we've had to prioritize the study of the Scriptures throughout the day and read about the heroes and history of our faith and other religions.

Home education can be used to promote spiritual growth no matter what your beliefs are. Daytime volunteering shifts, late worship services on a school night, midday prayer breaks, dropping everything to help a neighbor in need, vacations to study world religions in person—these are all realistic possibilities for home educators depending on their own priorities.

* * *

Homeschoolers are able to engage in deep, meaningful discussions right in the moment, nurturing the whole student, soul included.

* * *

Kids are naturally curious and wonderfully observant about life's biggest questions. I've often heard my own young kids and others pondering the same questions I recall discussing in my college philosophy classes. "Where do we go when we die?" Or, "How do you know you're not dreaming right now?" In my experience, they typically don't recognize it themselves, but kids are deep thinkers. Thankfully, homeschoolers do not have to check their spirituality outside the classroom door. They are able to engage in deep, meaningful discussions right in the moment, nurturing the whole student, soul included.

Your Homeschool, LLC

Personal edge, flexibility, and innovation are some of the key advantages enjoyed by small businesses. Because overhead costs are low and bureaucracy minimized, small businesses can react quickly to changing market conditions. Small business customers enjoy personalized attention to their unique needs, which often creates a deeper trust between customer and service provider. Additionally, smaller companies can try out new ideas and implement or discard them within a short time frame. These advantages allow small, local businesses to compete effectively not *despite* their small size but *because* of it.

Homeschooling parents are like entrepreneurs.

Although homeschools are much more than home-based tutoring businesses and are not in competition with larger educational institutions, other aspects of home education are analogous to the small business model. In many ways, homeschooling parents are like entrepreneurs. They have the freedom to innovate and cast a personalized vision for their family's education, modifying their approach as their kids grow and needs change. As the "business owners," parents have the greatest vested interest in the success of their venture and the decision-making power to effect positive change and growth.

Home educators have control over their own time, plus they can essentially gain back additional time through the efficiencies inherent in small-scale enterprises. Good ideas, curricula, and methods can be implemented immediately and ineffective ones thrown out just as quickly. Portions of work can be tackled in-house to save on expenses or outsourced to save on time. The time-money balance can be adjusted as needed, allowing homeschoolers to react nimbly to unexpected events and ever-changing seasons of life.

In a homeschool setting, parents can adjust their expectations and methods based on the unique needs and abilities of their family members. They can set priorities based on their "local customers" (that is, their own kids). Specific immediate goals for physical, intellectual, emotional, and spiritual wellness can be integrated daily, while, at the same time, progress can be made towards long-term individual and group goals. Just like small businesses, homeschools are successful not *despite* their uniqueness but *because* of it.

The Adventure Begins

Three generations in, the modern homeschooling movement is still often—unfortunately—misunderstood. Even its name is, in a way, a misnomer. In most cases, homeschool is not simply "school at home." It's an educational lifestyle *based* in the home and radiating outward. The potential opportunities and effectiveness of the method are great reasons to *start* homeschooling, not reasons why you *shouldn't*. And though it will be challenging at times, it's not impractical. Millions have done it successfully and you can, too!

If you'll indulge me in one last analogy, I've found that homeschooling is like buying a house. When I lived in an apartment, I enjoyed limited responsibility but also had limited control. The landlord took care of the plumbing problems and the landscaping, but I wasn't allowed to customize even so much as the paint color without permission. At the time, it fit my needs perfectly.

Homeschooling is an educational lifestyle based *in the home and radiating outward.*

Skipping forward a dozen years, my family purchased a single family detached home. Our responsibilities increased significantly, but so did our freedom. Being homeowners, we pay our taxes and follow the ordinances in our neighborhood, but we now enjoy relative autonomy when it comes to our home and property. If we want to plant daisies, renovate our bathroom, buy new carpet, or add a backyard sandbox for our kids, we're free to do so. We're the ones who take care of the leaky sink now, but we can decide when and how to get the job done. We're free to adjust the level of responsibility on our plate to match our current needs and abilities by outsourcing chores, such as lawn service or repairs, if needed.

Homeschooling is very much the same. By basing your kids' education at home, you will be adding (or, more accurately, *reclaiming*) a significant scope of work that the school system would otherwise be providing. You'll be the one finding curricula, signing up for a co-op, and deciding how often you want to go on field trips. You'll determine what aspects to do yourself and what to outsource, depending on your finances, time, and abilities.

--- ...

If you step onto the homeschooling path, your journey won't be easy but it will be worth it.

--- ...

Public (or private) school is what most of us know. It's often looked at as "normal" because it is, statistically speaking, the norm—the lifestyle of the majority. This can mistakenly imply that other choices are "abnormal" in a negative sense. But, of course, the legitimacy of an educational option should not be judged by where it falls on the "everybody's doing it" scale.

Bestselling author and clinical psychologist, Elaine N. Aron, PhD, reminds us, "There are so many legitimate ways to fill a life, by dedicating it to gaining knowledge, doing God's will, helping others, creative expression, new experiences, or family life and friendship."[139] *Many legitimate ways.* She urges parents not to "dismiss homeschooling as an option if it seems right for you, even if everyone around you disagrees. It is truly a highly individual matter."

---

139. Elaine N. Aron, *The Highly Sensitive Child* (New York, NY: Broadway Books, 2002), 243.

I couldn't agree more. And now that you have a fuller, more accurate picture of this educational alternative, you're better equipped to decide whether it's a good fit for your family. You're now "the boss" with "the info." You're the educated shopper with a choice to make. If you step onto the homeschooling path, your journey won't be easy but it will be worth it. You'll be the small business entrepreneur with a reason and a vision to keep you going on the hard days. You'll be the responsible first-time homebuyer, excited for the opportunities that lie ahead and resourceful enough to learn as you go and succeed.

We've come to the end of this book and analogies can only take us so far. In reality, you're the guardian of your child(ren), and it's your privilege and obligation to nurture their minds, bodies, and souls as they learn and grow. You know them better and love them more than anyone else in the world. I pray that the choices we all make for our kids' education are those that will cultivate a lifelong love of learning and help them achieve their purpose and highest potential in life. May God richly bless your journey.

What's Next?

Thank you for reading this book! Please consider leaving an Amazon review and sharing *Think About Homeschooling* on social media.

To learn more about homeschooling, subscribe to my blog, ***www.sensiblehomeschool.com***, where you'll find advice, encouragement, and practical tips for starting or continuing your home education adventure.

If you have questions about the book or about homeschooling, I'd love to hear from you! Email me at ***contact@sensiblehomeschool.com***.

Made in the USA
Columbia, SC
18 October 2021